MODERN JAPAN

A Volume in the Comparative Societies Series

MODERN JAPAN

A Volume in the Comparative Societies Series

HAROLD R. KERBO

JOHN A. MCKINSTRY
both of
California Polytechnic State University
San Luis Obispo

 **McGraw-Hill**

Boston, Massachusetts   Burr Ridge, Illinois   Dubuque, Iowa
Madison, Wisconsin   New York, New York
San Francisco, California   St. Louis, Missouri

McGraw-Hill

*A Division of The **McGraw·Hill** Companies*

Editorial director: *Phillip A. Butcher*
Sponsoring editor: *Jill Gordon*
Editorial coordinator: *Amy Smeltzley*
Marketing manager: *Sally Constable*
Project manager   *Kimberly Hooker*
Production supervisor: *Scott Hamilton*
Senior designer: *Laurie J. Entringer*
Compositor: *GAC/Shepard Poorman*
Typeface: *11/13 Palatino*
Printer: *R. R. Donnelley & Sons Company*

Library of Congress Cataloging-in-Publication Data

Kerbo, Harold R.
    Modern Japan / Harold R. Kerbo, John A. McKinstry.
        p.   cm.
    Includes index.
    ISBN 0–07–034426–4
    1. Japan.   I. McKinstry, John A.   II. Title
    DS806.K47   1998   97–35799

952.04—dc21

http://www.mhhe.com

EDITOR'S PREFACE

In one of the early scenes of the movie *Reds*, the U.S. revolutionary journalist John Reed, just back from covering the beginning of World War I, is asked by a roomful of business leaders, "What is this War really about?" John Reed stands, and stops all conversation with a one word reply—"profits." Today, war between major industrial nations would disrupt profits much more than create money for a military industrial complex. Highly integrated global markets and infrastructures support the daily life of suburban families in Chicago and urban squatter settlements in Bombay. These ties produce a social and economic ecology that transcends political and cultural boundaries.

The world is a very different place than it was for our parents and grandparents. Those rare epic events of world war certainly invaded their everyday lives and futures, but we now find that daily events thousands of miles away, in countries large and small, have a greater impact on North Americans than ever before, with the speed of this impact multiplied many times in recent decades. Our standard of living, jobs, and even prospects of living in a healthy environment have never before been so dependent on outside forces.

Yet, there is much evidence that North Americans have less easy access to good information about the outside world than even a few years ago. Since the end of the Cold War, newspaper and television coverage of events in other countries has dropped dramatically. It is difficult to put much blame on the mass media, however: international news seldom sells any more. There is simply less interest.

It is not surprising, then, that Americans know comparatively little about the outside world. A recent *Los Angeles Times* survey provides a good example: People in eight countries were asked five basic questions about current events of the day. Americans were dead last in their knowledge, trailing people from Canada, Mexico, England, France, Spain, Germany, and Italy.* It is also not surprising that the annual report published by the Swiss World Economic

---

*For example, while only 3 percent of Germans missed all five questions, 37 percent of the Americans did (*Los Angeles Times*, March 16, 1994).

Forum always ranks American executives quite low in their international experience and understanding.

Such ignorance harms American competitiveness in the world economy in many ways. But there is much more. Seymour Martin Lipset put it nicely in one of his recent books: "Those who know only one country know no country" (Lipset 1996: 17). Considerable time spent in a foreign country is one of the best stimulants for a sociological imagination: Studying or doing research in other countries makes us realize how much we really, in fact, have learned about our own society in the process. Seeing other social arrangements, ways of doing things, and foreign perspectives allows for far greater insight to the familiar, our own society. This is also to say that ignorance limits solutions to many of our own serious social problems. How many Americans, for example, are aware that levels of poverty are much lower in all other advanced nations and that the workable government services in those countries keep poverty low? Likewise, how many Americans are aware of alternative means of providing health care and quality education or reducing crime?

We can take heart in the fact that sociology in the United States has become more comparative in recent decades. A comparative approach, of course, was at the heart of classical European sociology during the 1800s. But as sociology was transported from Europe to the United States early in the twentieth century, it lost much of this comparative focus. In recent years, sociology journals have published more comparative research. There are large data sets with samples from many countries around the world in research seeking general laws on issues such the causes of social mobility or political violence, all very much in the tradition of Durkheim. But we also need much more of the old Max Weber: His was a qualitative historical and comparative perspective (Smelser 1976; Ragin and Zaret 1983). Weber's methodology provides a richer understanding of other societies, a greater recognition of the complexity of social, cultural, and historical forces shaping each society. Ahead of his time in many ways, C. Wright Mills was planning a qualitative comparative sociology of world regions just before his death in 1961 (Horowitz 1983: 324). Too few American sociologists have yet to follow in his footsteps.

Following these trends, sociology textbooks in the United States have also become more comparative in content in recent years. And while this tendency must be applauded, it is not enough. Typically there is an example from Japan here, another from Germany there, and so on haphazardly for a few countries in different subject areas as the writer's knowledge of these bits and pieces allows. What we need are the textbook equivalents of a richer Weberian comparative analysis, a qualitative comparative analysis of the social, cultural, and historical forces that have combined to make relatively unique societies around the world. It is this type of comparative material that can best help people in the United States overcome their lack of understanding about other countries and allow them to see their own society with much greater insight.

The Comparative Societies Series, of which this book is a part, has been designed as a small step in filling this need. We have currently selected 12 countries on which to focus: Japan, Thailand, Switzerland, Mexico, Eritria, Hungary, Germany, China, India, Iran, Brazil, and Russia. We selected these countries as representatives of major world regions and cultures, and each will be examined in separate books written by talented sociologists. All of the basic sociological issues and topics will be covered: Each book will begin with a look at the important historical and geographical forces shaping the society, then turn to basic aspects of social organization and culture. From there each book will proceed to examine the political and economic institutions of the specific country, along with the social stratification, the family, religion, education, and finally urbanization, demography, social problems, and social change.

Although each volume in the Comparative Societies Series is of necessity brief to allow for use as supplementary readings in standard sociology courses, we have tried to assure that this brief coverage provides students with sufficient information to better understand each society, as well as their own. The ideal would be to transport every student to another country for a period of observation and learning. Realizing the unfortunate impracticality of this ideal, we hope to do the next best thing—to at least mentally move these students to a country very different from their own, provide something of the everyday reality of the people in these other countries, and demonstrate how the tools of sociological analysis can help them see these societies as well as their own with much greater understanding.

Harold R. Kerbo
San Luis Obispo, CA
June 1997

Japan has always seemed a puzzle to most Americans and other Westerners. Japan is so modern, so industrialized, and yet, some-how so different. The countries of North America and Europe have their differences of course, as shown clearly in some of the other volumes in this Comparative Societies Series. But after working and living for several months in a European country such as Germany, it starts to feel more like home, the people in general become rather predictable and familiar to you, and eventually you can go about your daily routine without thinking much of being in a different country. Not so in Japan. After living and working for many months in Japan, you might think you have a routine, you might get through most of a day without thinking much about being in a foreign country, but then it hits you: every day something seems to happen, or you see something, that makes you sit back and think, to wonder why the people do things so differently.

Since Westerners had their first extensive contact with Japan they have been writing about the "exotic" Japanese people. Japan was not even known to exist among Europeans until the accounts of Marco Polo described "Chipangu," an island full of "idolaters" with "great amounts of gold" (Massarella 1990: 13). The first account in English that Japan existed came in 1577 with Richard Willie's *The History of Travayle in the West and East Indies* (Massarella 1990: 65). As we will see, it was not long after this that the new Tokugawa shogun (military rulers) closed the country to foreigners in the 1630s, restricting foreign contacts to a small island off the coast near Nagasaki. From then until the forced opening of Japan in 1853, the primary accounts of Japan came from Dutch merchants having contact with the Japanese on what came to be called the "Dutch Island." By the late 1800s, the West was getting somewhat more inside information about the Japanese culture and society from writers such as Lafcadio Hearn, an American journalist who had fallen in love with Japan, moved there permanently in 1890, and became the first Westerner allowed to take Japanese citizenship (Rosenstone 1988). In books such as *Kokoro: Hints and Echoes of the Japanese Inner Life, Glimpses of Unfamiliar Japan,*

Exotics and Retrospectives, and *In Ghostly Japan,* Hearn tells of the "real" Japan that is often "mysterious and strange" to the Western civilization.

By the early 1900s, when one of our sociological masters, Max Weber, was writing, there was at least some material on the Japanese society published in German, French, and English. Not only had Japan recently begun extensive contact with the West, but it was recognized as one of the emerging economic and military powers in Asia, especially after it defeated Russia in a short war during 1905. Among intellectuals in Europe, Japan was now becoming a curiosity, as suggested by Puccini's opera *Madam Butterfly* and the "Japonisme" fad among leading Western painters such as Monet, Girard, Manet, Degas, and Whistler.

Still, the new quantity of work and interest in Japan among Europeans at the turn of the century was not matched by quality and accuracy (Yawata 1963; Golzio 1985). As a result, in some of his writings Weber's several examples about Japan's possible economic development were simply wrong. He thought the prospects for economic development in Japan were dim, at least without massive help from the West. Weber did not even have some of the facts correct about economic development in Japan before the mid-nineteenth century, the nature of Japanese religion, or Japanese cities (Yawata 1963; Golzio 1985; Kerbo and Wittenhagen 1992).

Even more recently, during the late 1950s when it became evident that Japan would become an industrial power, many of the leading American sociologists (including people such as Talcott Parsons) had concluded that in the process of industrialization Japan would have to become more like "us"—modern Western societies. Now, after more than three decades, one of these sociologists has admitted "we were wrong" (Bellah 1985). Today it is evident that Japan has industrialized and modernized without becoming a copy of the West, and in fact the Western industrial nations have been trying to copy some of the more innovative aspects of Japan's modern economy.

We can no longer afford such inaccurate assumptions about Japan, or any country in Asia for that matter. (It is now clear, for example, that more knowledge among Americans about Vietnam's culture and society could have saved several thousands of lives [Jamieson 1995; Kamm 1996].) Early in the twenty-first century, more of the world's GNP will be concentrated in Asia than anywhere else. In their future careers, many American young people are likely to be working closely with people from Japan or other Asian countries. And because Japanese people know much more about the American society than Americans know about Japan, Americans are placed in a dangerous disadvantage.

In his novel, *Foreign Studies,* the respected contemporary Japanese writer, Shusaku Endo, tries to make the basic point that Japanese people and Westerners will never really know one another. After many years of studying in Paris, the Japanese characters in this novel could never come to understand and feel comfortable with Western attitudes or lifestyles, returning to Japan either merely pretending they have or simply feeling lost.

Endo's position, we argue, is too extreme. It may be the case that few if any Westerners will ever become completely "Japanized," or that few if any Japanese will ever become completely Westernized. Armed with deeper knowledge of the others' culture and society, however, people can better understand each other and successfully work together to a much greater degree than has been the case in the past.

The present book is one attempt to achieve this goal. Although several books in recent years have addressed themes of Japanese culture and society, to our knowledge this book is the first to consistently consider all of the main sociological issues with respect to the Japanese society and culture. Chapter 1, "The Place, the People, and the Past," begins with some of the basics about geography, characteristics of the people, and Japanese history. Chapter 2, "Japanese Culture and Social Structure," covers what we think are some of the most important aspects of Japanese culture and social organization that Westerners must know to understand Japan more fully. Chapters 3 through 6, on the Japanese political system, economy, social stratification, and power elites, cover what we think Westerners must know about how the government and economic institutions operate in Japan and how the system of ranking is in some ways quite different from what Westerners experience. Chapters 7 through 10 examine other basic characteristics of the Japanese society and culture: the family, religion, education, and Japanese urban life. Finally, Chapters 11 and 12 present some of the most important social problems facing Japan and discuss the changes that Japan must confront as it moves into the twenty-first century.

We are perfectly aware that this present volume does not provide Westerners with everything they need to know about the Japanese society and culture. But we believe it makes a start. We have included references to many more specialized books and articles about Japan throughout this book, and we have included a list of many Web sites where other current information about Japan can be located. If our readers finish this book feeling that Japan seems a little less mysterious, a little more understandable, we have accomplished our job. And along the way, we also hope our readers become quite interested in Japan, as we have over the years. If this is the case, our work will have been rewarding indeed.

Harold R. Kerbo
John A. McKinstry

References

Horowitz, Irving Louis. *C. Wright Mills: An American Utopian*. New York: Free Press, 1983.

Lipset, Seymour Martin. *American Exceptionalism: A Double-Edged Sword*. New York: W.W. Norton, 1996.

Ragin, Charles; and David Zaret. "Theory and Method in Comparative Strategies." *Social Forces* 61 (1983), pp. 731–54.

Smelser, Neil J. *Comparative Methods in the Social Sciences*. Englewood Cliffs, NJ: Prentice Hall, 1976.

CONTENTS

Chapter 4

The Japanese Economy   47

Chapter 5

Social Stratification in Japan   59

Chapter 6

The Japanese Power Elite   75

Chapter 11

Social Problems in Modern Japan   141

Chapter 12

Social Change and Japan in the Twenty-First Century: A Conclusion   161

NORTH KOREA

Vladivostok

Yuzhno Sakhalinsk

Sapporo

Pyongyang

Seoul

Sendai

Incheon

JAPAN

SOUTH KOREA

Taejeon

Taegu

Sakai-minato

Nagoya

Tokyo

Chiba

Pusan

Kyoto

Hiroshima

Osaka

Kita-kyushu

Fukuoka

CHAPTER 1
The Place, the People, and the Past

In one sense, human societies are like individual human beings: Individuals are influenced by their environments and by events that happen in their lives. But although it is often possible to perceive and even to predict the effects of these factors, individuals subject to identical environmental and historical conditioning, siblings for example, often end up with completely different personalities. And so it is with societies. Effects of some environmental factors are fairly obvious. For example, the Japanese have a very healthy curiosity about the non-Japanese world, but at the same time they tend to harbor attitudes that make it difficult for them to open up to a wider social reality. The United States, in turn, is a place where people become intimate very quickly, using first names almost at once and visiting the interior of homes of people they have just met. Both traits are forged to a great deal by geography: in Japan by the relative isolation of their homeland before the modern period, and in the United States by the broad expanses of territory, which dictated that people were often set down among strangers at a time of life when they had to learn to interact quickly to survive. However, no amount of information about geography, history, physical characteristics, or anything else can ever give us a complete explanation of why a particular society is the way it is. The best we can do is learn about these things and use them as a framework, slowly filling in a more complete

1

picture the only way we can, by examining the important features of a society one by one. We begin with the basic elements of the framework: the geography of Japan, general characteristics of the Japanese people, and brief outline of Japanese history.

THE PLACE

Japan consists of a series of four large islands and a few much smaller islands off the coast of the Asian mainland between latitudes 30 and 45 degrees north. As you can see from the map, the whole of Japan is made up of rather narrow stretches of land—no place in the entire nation is more than 75 miles from the sea; but the Japanese archipelago runs quite far from northeast to southwest, with a range of about 1,700 miles. In climate, the long series of islands that constitute Japan is similar to the east coast of the United States, with Japan's northernmost island of Hokkaido comparable to New England. Summers in Hokkaido are shorter and milder than further south, and winters are long and cold; there is even glacial ice in the ocean off the north coast of the island in the winter months. The large middle island of Honshu together with the smallest of all the larger islands, Shikoku, have a climate something like the area from New York to Washington, with four full seasons including some hot summer days and perhaps a little snow in winter. Further south, Kyushu is somewhat similar to North and South Carolina; and finally, a few hundred miles further to the south, Okinawa is reminiscent of southern Florida, with the same kind of beaches beckoning northern tourists from November through March.

Something that greatly distinguishes Japan from the U.S. east coast, however, is terrain. As a string of mountain ranges pushed up above sea level by volcanic activity, Japan is in a geological sense very young. The rough mountainous terrain of Japan has not had enough time to wear down, and so there is comparatively little flat land anywhere. In fact, the country is so mountainous that wheeled vehicles were never used in Japan until its railway system was developed about 150 years ago; there was simply not enough level land to develop a road system suitable for carriages.

The Japanese customarily think of their nation as a small place, and in comparison with the United States, which including Alaska is about 26 times larger, it does seem small. But Japan, with 124,000 square miles of territory, is larger than the average nation. It is larger, for example, in landmass than Italy or Germany and larger than the entire British Isles, including Ireland. There is little doubt, however, that Japan does suffer from a land shortage. Even if the nation were not so mountainous, with a population of about 125 million, a little less than half that of the United States and twice that of Britain, Japan would have less land to go around than most other countries. What makes the situation worse is that most of the population has to be packed together in small coastal plains; the interior of the country is simply too rugged for urban development or even for most agriculture. The metropolitan area around Tokyo, usually called *kantō chihō* or the Kanto region, is smaller than the Los Angeles basin and has a population of around 20 million, just under five times that of the Los Angeles area. It is not surprising that with that kind of population density in major urban areas, residential units tend to be smaller than in most nations, and the Japanese have had to learn to use land with great care. Farms in most parts of Japan are only a few acres in size and seem more like large gardens to foreigners. They are intensively worked and, in spite of their small size, are among the most productive per acre in the world.

Although short on flat land and lacking the resources of many other nations, Japan does have plenty of coastline. Because the country has more access to the ocean than many larger nations such as the United States, the sea has been and continues to be extremely important in lives of Japanese people. For a long time, coastal boats have been a major form of transportation in the mountainous country, and the Japanese take more food from the sea than any other people.

THE PEOPLE

The Japanese consider themselves to be a separate race, and it certainly is true that the people present and past who live on those islands have been interbreeding for thousands of years, evolving physical characteristics that are different in some very small respects from other north Asians such as the Koreans or Mongolians. Most scholars who study the subject think the Japanese are made up of a mixture of racial ingredients (Sansom 1958; Befu 1981; Sahara 1987; Reischauer 1988). It is quite obvious that people in Japan are basically of East Asian origin, with most of the genetic inheritance coming from north Asia, probably by waves of tribal people who came to the Japanese islands through the Korean peninsula sometime between 4,000 to 5,000 years ago. There is general agreement, however, that the Japanese are not pure East Asian, but actually a mixture of mainly East Asian with at least two other racial types. Several hundred years before the large infusion of population from north Asia, people similar in racial type and culture to present-day Pacific Island people such as Micronesians and original Taiwanese, people of darker skin and wavier hair than north Asians and without the characteristic Asian eye shape, drifted into the islands. Remnants of this part of Japan's antecedents can still be seen in the country's domestic architecture, with light wooden prototypes not seen anywhere else in the northern part of the Asian region. Of course, the early people left some of their genes as well; the range of physical appearance in Japan, more than in China or Korea, includes many people who could fit unnoticed with a group of Pacific Islanders.

The third and smallest of the mixture of three racial types is with the aboriginal population of the islands. Not very much is known about where this group originally came from or even when they arrived, but it is believed that they predate the two larger immigrations by at least several hundred years. They were short in stature, did not have the typical Asian epicanthic eye shape, and had much more body and facial hair than East Asians. There are still a few descendants of these aboriginal people of Japan, called Ainu, who live mainly in the southern part of Hokkaido. The fact that Japanese today on average have more body hair than other Asians and men in Japan have the ability to grow fuller beards than most other Asians is usually attributed to a small strain of aboriginal admixture in the Japanese gene pool (Sansom 1958).

There are of course several different ways nations can be compared and classified. Currently about 200 societies in the world are sufficiently large enough and autonomous enough to qualify as nations. If we examine these 200 nations carefully, we uncover many social and cultural aspects that distinguish them from each other and other aspects that render each of them to be similar to other societies. In comparing Japan with other industrial nations of the modern world, we can see how societies can be both very different and quite similar at the same time. The level of economic development of societies by itself is a powerful determinant of the way people live their lives (Lenski, Lenski, and Nolan 1991). The overwhelming majority of the nearly 200 nations of the world are poor in economic terms, and while all of them include people with advanced education and high standards of living, those kinds of people are part of a small elite sector of the population, not representative of average citizens. There are relatively few nations in which ordinary people enjoy high standards of living. Japan is one of them along with a couple of dozen other societies such as the United States.

In a sociological sense, a list of the ways the vast majority of Americans and the vast majority of Japanese are similar is fairly long. To begin with, both societies have a large **middle class.** By world standards, average people in both places eat well, dress well, know a lot, travel a great deal both within and outside the nation, and share, along with the rest of the economically advanced nations, the fruits of a highly developed and widely dispersed technology. An average Japanese person might well find it easier to stay for a time in an American household than in, for example, a typical Chinese household. The modern world of advanced nations has to a considerable degree produced a common culture, at least on a superficial level, sharing much of the same hardware and spending time doing many of the same things.

Both Japanese and Americans give over a third of their young people some kind of formal education beyond high school, the highest of any two large nations in the world. Both complain about government a lot, but people in neither society need live in fear of it, and both receive expansive and expert services from all levels of government that they tend to take for granted. Survey research reveals that most people in both societies, while recognizing that their nation has difficult problems, consider it the best place to live in the world.

But of course there are significant ways in which Japanese and Americans are different, and in fact Japan is somewhat set apart from all the other nations of the economically developed world.

The Industrial Revolution was the starting point of modern economic development, and the nations earliest to be affected by that historical phenomenon are still the leading economic powers. The modern economic system began in Europe, and for more than a hundred years only European societies were part of it (Wallerstein 1974, 1980, 1989). Europeans saw themselves as leaders of a new world order based on economic power, which ultimately translated into military power. This was the mentality that produced the system of European colonialism; the characteristics of European culture and history were often widely assumed to be necessary for joining the club of rich and powerful nations.

Japan destroyed those notions forever. For the first time in history, a nation traveled a completely different route into the top level of industrial powers. Japan proved to the world that a nation need not be European, trace its civilized roots from classical Greece or Rome, or have any significant connection to Christianity to become a fully developed industrial society. The significance of all this will be stressed a bit more in the following chapters on the political and economic institutions of Japan.

THE PAST

As far as civilizations go, Japan does not have a truly ancient history. Unlike its neighbor China, which was one of the original cradles of civilization and traces its history as far back as 4,000 years, the history of Japan is about as old as the history of Britain. On the basis of available evidence, we can divide Japanese history roughly into five periods covering all together about 1,600 years. And because social and cultural change has tended to speed up in recent centuries, the closer we get to the present, the shorter these periods become. The first of these, from about AD 400 to around 1200, was a time of copying and importing elements from China and of changing these elements and molding them around native themes to form a distinctive tradition. The second period, lasting from roughly 1200 to just prior to 1600 was the time when Japan was characterized by almost nonstop civil war between rival states, small independent territories controlled by warlord families. During this period, the *samurai*, an elite group of military professionals, came to center stage, and some of the starker forms of Japanese culture—zen, the tea ceremony, ritual suicide—grew to maturity. Third, from 1600 until 1868, the entire nation was united under the control of a single ruling family, called the *shogun*. Japan was cut off from the outside world during that period and in technological terms became frozen in time. Fourth, the period from 1868 until defeat in World War II in 1945 can be considered a single period of Japanese history; it was during that time that Japan modernized and became an imperialistic military power. Finally, from 1945 to the present, Japan has followed a path similar to other advanced capitalist nations in nourishing authentically democratic institutions and providing a high standard of living for its citizens. We should now take a closer look at each of these periods.

The Classical Period: 400–1200

Ancient China was the only civilized tradition that the pre-civilized Japanese people had any contact with, and it was from China that the core of what was to form a Japanese version of Asian civilization came. Many elements of this civilization can still be seen today. Borrowing from China began for the Japanese in the fifth century AD and continued for 300 years or so. Following this period of intense importation of Chinese ways, Japan began a process of digesting Chinese artifacts and turning some of them into native patterns, producing a purely Japanese application of the original imports. The written language is a good example. The Japanese adopted the nonphonetic Chinese writing system, something not easy because the Japanese and Chinese languages are extremely different in both structure and sound. For several centuries the Japanese simply continued to speak their own language and wrote in Chinese, much as medieval Europeans spoke current modes of languages such as French or German and wrote everything in a version of Latin. Space considerations preclude a detailed explanation of the characteristics of Japanese language, but we can say that the result of imposing a Chinese prototype on their own language has resulted in a written language that undoubtedly is the most difficult to learn of any system since passing of the ancient Egyptian civilization. This renders even more impressive the literacy rate of Japan, one of the highest in the world.

Japan borrowed much, but all the while it remained distinct as a society, not becoming merely part of China. Geography was mostly responsible for that important sense of distinctness from the rich civilized tradition on the East Asia mainland. Not until much later, until the fifteenth century, was China ever much of a seafaring power, with Japan just far enough away to be left alone. What Japan got from China it got because some people in Japan wanted it. Nothing from the outside was ever forced on the society. Imported ways of doing things brought in from China, and later on things brought in from the West, have always been seen by the Japanese as interesting additions to older native ways, and somehow, the older native ways in Japan are more likely than in other places to be honored and preserved along with the imports (Varley 1977). With respect to all of the above, it is also significant to note that of the East Asian nations only Japan and Thailand were never colonized.

The institution of emperor is a good example of mixing imported elements of culture with Japanese ways. The emperor in China was conceived of as the pinnacle of Chinese society. The rule of his family line was rationalized, as was the case in traditional Europe, as divinely sanctioned. On the other hand, there has always been something very different in the way the Chinese and Japanese defined and reacted to their emperors. Chinese throughout their long history have been aware that the reign of an imperial lineage comes and goes, and the bloodline of emperors has been replaced by a new lineage many times. Japan may not be as old as China, but the bloodline of her imperial family has been far more durable than any of the Chinese dynasties.

Actually the origin of the Japanese imperial family is not exactly known. There seems to have been only one, and it begins well before written records were kept in Japan (Reischauer 1988). In fact, however, emperors of Japan have almost never in recorded history been real rulers. They have been in a way something much more important. Right up to the twentieth century, the emperor of Japan was accepted by a majority of Japanese as a direct connection with divinity itself, a manifestation of the most powerful *kami*, the supernatural force that resides in spirits and nature and is the foundation of the Shinto religion. Japanese emperors have played a role that could be described as high priests of an entire people, situated above the concerns of the secular world and political conflicts.

During this classical period, the Japanese developed their own homegrown version of literacy as well as fine arts and architecture that, although again undeniably inspired by Chinese prototypes, had more and more a truly Japanese flavor about them. Around the year 1000 a long narrative novel based on life at the imperial court was written by a woman named Shikibu. This book, *The Tale of Genji*, is over 1,000 pages in length in the original unedited version, written entirely in Japanese phonetic script. Its descriptions of people and events are vivid and sophisticated enough to hold the interest of readers through the centuries, and a shortened version is still widely read today.

The Period of Feudal Warfare: 1200–1600

Following the period of intense borrowing from China, Japan in the eleventh and twelfth centuries became once more rather isolated from the mainland of Asia. In the provinces, the authority of the government that ruled in the name of the emperor in what was then the capital city of Kyoto gave way to military struggle. The civil wars continued off and on in most parts of the country for several hundred years, creating one of the most warlike cultures ever known. A social system developed that was very similar to European **feudalism,** with castle towns dominating a surrounding countryside forming a kind of fief, what really amounted to a miniature kingdom. These fiefs were often fierce rivals, and the endless civil wars of this period were all about which rival chieftain would dominate over the fiefs in his area. People who did the actual fighting evolved into a kind of Japanese version of feudal knights who practiced their fighting skills all of their formative years and very often met death in combat in their 20s. As you know, they were called *samurai;* and Japanese literature, and more recently Japanese television and movies, fell hopelessly in love with them, as Hollywood once embraced the Western gunslinger as the epitome of courage and masculine virtue. Swordsmanship, and even more so, the technology of sword making, reached levels never seen before or since.

But during all of this mayhem, throughout this period of mass and protracted carnage, no emperor was ever in any danger. The emperor's residence for a thousand years before it was brought to the former shogun's palace in present-day Tokyo was in Kyoto. Unlike palaces of the warlords with their thick walls of heavy stone and systems of moats, some of which are still in place, the walls around the emperor's palace were never more than about 15 feet high, built of adobe and wood for privacy rather than for protection. It did not occur to those struggling for military advantage that anything could be gained by harming the emperor (Reischauer 1988). Today, royalty of Europe and elsewhere have given up the power to rule and have become symbols of national unity and a connection to history. In a way, the Japanese were ahead of their time during the past 1,000 years. Modern politics and governance have not forced the Japanese emperor to give up anything. That is exactly the way the role of emperor has always functioned in Japan.

Much of the interior of Japan consists of rugged mountainous terrain like this scene from the area called the Japan Alps in Nagano Prefecture.

The Edo Period: 1600–1868

During the final three decades of the sixteenth century, the civil wars were brought to a halt by an alliance of military strongmen under the leadership of a single ruler. There were actually three of these men in succession: The first two, Nobunaga Oda and Hideyoshi Toyotomi, while managing to gain dominance over all other groups and rule over a nation united as a single entity, were not able to create a system of stable transfer of power when they died. The third in line, Ieyasu Tokugawa, turned his considerable ability toward just that problem and built a dynasty of secular authority that lasted for two and a half centuries.

Ieyasu Tokugawa ruled far from the historic capital of Kyoto, building a palace bit by bit on the grounds of a tiny castle near the sea more than 200 miles to the east, in a place called Yoyogi, near the village of Edo. There wasn't much there to begin with, but within a hundred years, Edo was transformed into a thriving city larger than Kyoto, and another hundred years would see it grow into one of the largest cities of the world. What caused this virtual explosion in size, beyond the fact that it was the seat of all real political power in the land, was one of the most clever devices ever used to keep a regime in power. It was called *sankin kōtai,* often rendered in English as "alternate residence," but actually a hostage system applied to all of the more than 200 warlords of Japan, many of which had been bitter enemies of the Tokugawa family. Each warlord, called *daimyo* in Japanese, was forced to reside for half the year in a mansion in the new city of Edo, under the noses of the Tokugawa shogun's samurai. His parents, children, and all other close relatives had to stay back in his own palace while he was in Edo, and when he returned to tend to affairs of his own realm during the rest of the year, family members had to take his place in the Edo mansion. In this way, either the *daimyo* himself or close family members were always in hostage to the shogun's military forces. *Sankin kōtai* not only prevented military uprisings against the regime, it also forced the richest people in the land to live in the new city, attracting many of the best artisans from Kyoto and elsewhere to serve them in what would become Tokyo.

Many art forms and systems of entertainment gravitated to such a large number of elite people, but probably the most significant force driving the culture of Edo was the burgeoning merchant class. By the time Japan was opened up to the outside world and the

11   The Place, the People, and the Past

Tokugawa regime came to an end, there were perhaps more things to buy and more things to do in Edo than in any other city on earth.

Another notable aspect to the period of Tokugawa rule from 1600 to 1868, often called the Edo period, was something called in Japanese *sakoku rei*, the series of laws closing off Japan and rendering it isolated from all other nations. In the previous century, during the 1500s, Europeans, and especially Christian missionaries, had played a part in the intrigue between powerful military alliances. The Tokugawa regime was determined to put a stop to what it considered a danger to its exclusive power. Christianity was banned, and eventually Japanese were prohibited to leave the country and no foreigner was allowed to enter.

Although each daimyo had to collect taxes and manage his own realm virtually as a local ruler, nearly every aspect of the nation was scrutinized and controlled by rules laid down by the central government in Edo. Each daimyo's realm, called *han* in Japanese, was measured by how much rice was produced each year by peasants of the han. Likewise, such things as the size of the mansion required as residence in Edo, the number of military retainers allowed by the daimyo, and the size of the retinue accompanying the daimyo back and forth from Edo to his han were all precisely spelled out according to the amount of rice produced in that particular han (Reischauer 1988).

The Tokugawa regime planned a society in which a small military elite, closed to the rest of society by heredity, would have exclusive power over everyone else. In many ways, they created a system of social stratification a bit like the Indian caste system. All other people were ranked by occupation below the samurai elite, and each rank was inherited and in theory could not be changed. Peasants were ranked just below the samurai because it was their labor that produced the basic element in an agricultural society. Next came artisans, the people who served mainly the samurai by making all the artifacts they needed to live and to symbolize their elite status. Finally, at the bottom, officially ranked just above a group of outcastes, were the merchants, seen by the regime as parasites who served the least important function in society.

Not all samurai commanded great power. Daimyo in charge of very large han were counted in the samurai class, but many lower-ranked samurai were nothing more than professional guards with no real power at all. They received no pay for their services; in fact, it was undignified for a samurai, until near the end of the Edo period, to even handle money. But even the lowest-ranked samurai were completely set apart from all other Japanese by costume and manner. Only samurai could wear silk and carry weapons, and all others had to speak to them with special honorific language. They lived in castles, removed from ordinary people, and of course counted themselves as far superior to all those ranked beneath the samurai class (Sansom 1958).

As we know, real life has a way of following its own course, ignoring in many cases the path laid down by rule makers. This carefully planned system of a small elite ruling over an unchanging agricultural society was in time countermanded by the growth of power of the lowest-ranked group of all, the merchants. The samurai as a class continued to hold all political power, but the peace the Tokugawa regime so successfully enforced created an excellent environment for commerce, and it was the merchants who actually benefited most from the Tokugawa organization of society. The regime tried all sorts of ways to limit the growing power of merchants and their money, such as the rule limiting the number of unrelated people who could engage in a single enterprise, but try as they may, the role played by merchants in a slowly developing capitalist system continued to eat away at the central position the samurai were supposed to represent.

Many daimyo, and even the regime itself, came to be in debt to people with this new kind of power in Japan—the power of great wealth. Farmers, who were supposed to stay farmers, flocked to rapidly developing urban centers of Edo, Osaka, and Nagoya. They took jobs with the thousands of small businesses springing up everywhere. As proud as the samurai were, marriage between samurai and merchant families was not at all uncommon during the later stages of the period. As the merchant class grew in size and wealth, it could serve itself, and not just the samurai; merchants became the super-consumers of Japan. Everything money can buy flourished in urban Japan during the Edo period; whereas back at the castles, things went on pretty much as before—bastions of a warrior caste with no wars to fight.

In the cities, publishing of various kinds probably surpassed any society in Europe of the time. All kinds of entertainment, with a new, rich audience, became professionalized and reached very high standards. Artisans, who in theory were to produce products for the samurai, themselves became capitalists and, in spite of the rather simple technology of Japan then, made wares as fine in quality as anywhere in the world.

The Meiji Period, 1868–1912, The Beginning of Modern Japan

All this buying, selling, and making of things was in a society that had never seen a steam engine, that did not possess machinery of any kind, that had no cannons or other modern military weapons, that had no seagoing vessels, and in which virtually all the documents of government were written by hand—and this was as late as 150 years ago. As a society cut off from the outside world by order of its own government, Japan missed the Industrial Revolution.

It is interesting to speculate how long the country would have gone on this way. Many observers think it would not have been long because discontent with the social order was beginning to rise in the group that mattered most in issues of politics—among the samurai class itself.

In 1853, an event occurred that brought discontent to a fever pitch and, although it took 15 years to finally come about, was the ultimate cause of the collapse of the Tokugawa regime. Several nations had made contact with the shogun's representatives in an effort to open Japan's ports, but it was an American fleet that finally forced an audience with the shogun by sailing in unannounced to the very gates of the shogun's palace in Edo. The Tokugawa regime had taken over rule of Japan by force and continued to rule by threat of military force. When it was shown to be powerless in keeping out the intruders, the image held so long of an all-powerful regime evaporated.

The few years following the American visit was a time of widespread discussion, and there was a great deal of pondering the future of the nation. Finally, an alliance of samurai from han that had never been favored by the Tokugawa regime organized a military overthrow of the entire shogunate system, replacing it with a completely new system. In the new government, the emperor, so long merely a religious figurehead in Kyoto, was brought to Edo, which was renamed Tokyo and made the official capital of the nation. The emperor was to serve as a symbol in uniting the people into a modern, European-style nation. The emperor had no more real power than before, but as a symbol, the role of emperor was greatly enhanced. The emperor in the new nation was the theoretical head of state, and everything was done in his name. The men who actually ran the country, former samurai from the han who led the rebellion against the shogun, together with some court nobles from Kyoto, formed a kind of behind-the-scenes ruling committee. There was a legislative body, but at first it had little power, only gaining in significance after 1900 when political parties were formed and voting for legislative representatives was expanded.

Japan's period of opening up to the larger world and the feverish and spectacular process of modernization that followed all happened during the Meiji period. It was a period that saw as much fundamental change in a single generation than experienced by the people of any large social system in recorded history. One way Japan modernized was in military technology and strategy it copied from the major Western powers. It was successful enough in this to defeat a much larger Chinese military force in the first of its modern wars, the Sino-Japanese War of 1894–95, and 10 years later it was able to defeat a European power, imperial Russia, in its second modern war. That victory was extremely significant; it forced Europe and America to recognize Japan as a peer, the first non-Western society to join the club of economic and military leaders.

During the Meiji period, the Japanese transformed themselves into students of the Western world. Young former samurai were sent in groups to every economically advanced country of that time to learn all they could about how a modern society works. One can imagine the hardships they encountered; few spoke more than a few words of any Western language, and of course coming as they were out of a long period of forced isolation, they knew virtually nothing of life outside Japan. But these young men had a keen sense of purpose, and they were well aware of what was at stake. If Japan remained technologically backward, it would be swallowed up by the expansion of European power.

They returned to Japan with information about a wide variety of technological and administrative processes, from shipbuilding to police work, from military hardware and strategy to railroad engineering and power looms. The groups of young Japanese men were sent to specific societies that seemed to do particular things well. They went to England to study modern factory design and function, to Germany to learn about how to run a modern government, to the United States to learn about rail systems.

Japan also tried to lure experts of all kinds to come to Japan and teach them modern ways on their own soil. This was difficult to achieve because Japan had few amenities foreigners demanded. At great expense they carefully copied house design in Western cities so they could build housing that foreigners coming to Japan would accept. To get foreign experts to come to Japan for extended periods— and frankly not many did in the early years of Meiji—the Japanese offered salaries 10 to 20 times what professional Japanese were paid, often double the salaries Westerners could make if they stayed at home.

The Japanese made many mistakes in their passion for modernization, and there were many in Japan who suffered because of the effort. But as we will see in coming chapters, in the end the entire project produced the most rapid and complete material transformation of any society in history. By the early twentieth century, Japan in many ways resembled the societies of Europe more than it did any other Asian society. Not only did Japan have railroads, shipyards, and a modern military with up-to-date hardware by that time, but the hardware for all these things was produced in Japan by Japanese designers and Japanese workers. It would be many decades before any other Asian nation could make that claim.

CONCLUSION

The elongated shape of Japan is analogous in size and climate to the eastern seaboard of the United States, but in other ways it is more reminiscent of Switzerland, with sharply rising mountains forming a spine down the entire length of the nation. A population of close to 125 million is packed together in small coastal plains, making Japan far more crowded than its 124,000 square miles of territory might otherwise suggest.

The Japanese race is less purely north Asian than that of Korea or north China, with admixtures from the Pacific Islands and an aboriginal race with more European than Asian features. Not much in detail is known about the Japanese people until they acquired writing from the Chinese in the fifth century AD. A period of intense borrowing from Chinese civilization commenced about that time, lasting for about 500 years. The Japanese adopted the Chinese writing system, a system of emperor-based government, a form of architecture, and much of the hardware of Chinese culture. Because the Japanese had relatively little physical contact with the Chinese, they gradually altered the things they borrowed to suit their own tastes and ways.

Beginning in the middle of the fourteenth century, the Japanese islands gradually began to decentralize into small warring ministates. Wars between these states were being fought somewhere in Japan continuously for more than two centuries, finally being brought to an end with the unification of the entire country under the authority of the Tokugawa family. The Tokugawa regime established peace over the land and formally isolated Japan from contact with the outside world for nearly 250 years. During this period, which lasted until 1868, the merchant class, theoretically the lowest in what was supposed to be a rigid hierarchy of inherited status, benefited more than any other group, giving rise to the first wave of Japanese capitalism.

Forced isolation kept Japan backward at a time when Europe and America were forging ahead as technological and military powers. Finally Japan was forced to open to the outside world by the U.S. navy, and the shock of the forced opening led, within 15 years, to an overthrow of the Tokugawa regime. A new government structure was put into place with a new and expanded role for the emperor as the shogun's palace became the imperial palace and the surrounding city renamed Tokyo, "eastern capital." The new leaders of Japan were determined to catch up with the West to avoid being dominated by its superior technology. The first three decades of the new Meiji regime, 1870 to 1900, saw Japan transformed into a modern industrial society, the most rapid such transition ever achieved.

CHAPTER 2

Japanese Culture and Social Structure

Many types of Japanese rituals and traditional practices stand out to Westerners visiting the country for the first time. These little differences might seem interesting but of no real significance when given only passing examination. For example, one thing learned quickly is that Japanese people find business cards very important. These cards are exchanged with much ritual; a bow and handing the card to another person in the proper manner is required, with the card left clearly on the table for a long time where it appears to be studied with care by the person receiving it. Another ritual learned quickly is that shoes must be taken off before entering someone's home and often also a place of business. And finally we can note the common practice of Japanese employees going out often with their co-workers after working hours to drink heavily and perhaps spend hours singing in a karaoke bar.

Uninformed Westerners might consider such traditions and behavior interesting if not strange; they might even consider some in a negative light, as in the case of our last example. But what might seem minor differences compared to Western behavior can often involve very important *cultural traditions* or differences in *social structure*. In the case of business cards, the strong tendency toward status ranking in Japan makes them necessary so that strangers first coming together know their respective ranks, and thus how to talk to each other, and even when and where to sit. Also, taking off one's shoes in a Japanese home is related to more than just keeping the floors clean: the tradition is related to a concept of "inside versus outside" and keeping the outside from spoiling the valued inside (Hendry 1987). Finally, the important practice of drinking with co-workers frequently after hours is related to the importance of solidarity within the group and making the work group a stronger reference group than Westerners would like to accept.

In this chapter we will examine key aspects of Japanese culture and social structure that provide important background information for understanding many other things about the Japanese society. We will consider such things as the collectivist value orientation of Japan, the importance of the group, the extent and means of maintaining conformity in Japan, and the important concept of insider versus outsider in the Japanese society.

CULTURAL EXPLANATIONS AND THEIR PROBLEMS

Many differences found in Japan, when compared to Western societies, are no doubt related to what is usually, and loosely, called **culture.** Other differences are often related to aspects of **social structure,** or how people and groups are tied together in the society. In regard to Japan it is often said that a value system emphasizing the group leads to more cooperation, self-sacrifice, economic strength, and a relative lack of many social problems compared to in the United States. This group orientation is then commonly explained with reference to religious principles from Buddhism, Confucianism, and Shintoism that are found in Japan's history.

Having said all of this, though, we must be cautious. First, cultural values are rather vague; in practice they need interpretation to show how they apply. Second, cultural values are sometimes subject to change and are not so deeply ingrained within individuals and societies as is often assumed. There has been much more change in Japanese history than most accounts have indicated. For example, much about the Japanese economy that is admired, such as lifetime employment, low inequality between managers and workers, and practices promoting teamwork, did not exist before World War II. These things cannot be primary aspects of Japanese culture if they have existed less than 50 years.

It is also very easy to exaggerate what are described as cultural features of any society. All cultural systems are complex and inconsistent; the very opposite tendency can often be seen existing right alongside the cultural feature being explained. For example, Americans are usually described as placing great emphasis on the individual; conversely, Japan is usually described as a place where personal identity is found more as part of a group. In many important ways these descriptions are valid, but as you will learn from Chapter 7, within marriage, Japanese spouses are actually much more independent than Americans, who, far more than Japanese, tend to merge their identities together as married couples. It is also interesting to observe that traditionally the "group-oriented" Japanese never had any team sports. All athletic and sporting events—archery, sumo wrestling, judo—involved individuals performing or competing without being members of teams. It wasn't until late in the nineteenth century that they finally got their first team sport—baseball—from those die-hard individualists, the Americans.

With these cautions in mind, however, we can look at some of the most general aspects of Japanese cultural values and social structure that do influence the society, the behavior of Japanese people, and much of what happens in Japan today.

ASIAN VALUE SYSTEMS

At the most general level of value preferences, the West is commonly described as having an **individualistic value system,** whereas Asia is described as having a **collectivist value system.** Most simply, this means that the group is more important in Asia and the individual is more important in the West (Smith 1983). Not all Western countries are alike with values such as individualism, nor are all Asian countries alike with respect to collectivism. But as such generalities go, this one tends to be quite valid. In his famous study of about 15,000 people from 53 countries, for example, Hofstede (1991) found the United States to score a 91 on his individualism index (100 is a perfect score) to be number one; Japan scored 46. Australia, England, Canada, the Netherlands, and New Zealand ranked just below the United States on this index, and countries such as Thailand, Singapore, Hong Kong, South Korea, Taiwan, and Malaysia scored even lower than Japan.

As industrialization was rapidly changing European societies in the eighteenth and nineteenth centuries, many of the best social scientists of the time—such as Émile Durkheim, Max Weber, and Ferdinand Tönnies—were speculating about how societies would survive; the previously strong bonds linking individuals to small groups in preindustrial societies were breaking as people became more mobile, thus leaving small villages for big cities. These scientists knew that a totally individualistic society, one with everyone going his or her own way, considering only his or her own selfish interests, would not work; there would be only destructive conflict and anarchy. However flawed some of his ideas, the great interpreter of the Western mind, Sigmund Freud, also outlined this dilemma of human societies in one of his greatest books, *Civilization and Its Discontents*, in 1930. Some means of organization and compromise must be attained between the conflicting interests of the group and the individual.

The Western industrialized societies evolved toward allowing ever more freedom to the individual. The individual, of course, must continue to have responsibilities toward, and even make some sacrifices for, important groups—the family and work groups, for example. But as much as possible, in these Western nations, and to the greatest extent in the United States,[1] value preferences suggest that individuals should be given as much freedom and independence as possible. Asian collectivist cultures, in contrast, require more sacrifice for group needs, placing more restraints on what the individual may do in satisfying individual desires. All of this not only affects the individual's relation to small groups, but also the individual's relation to the broader community and nation. As we will see in coming chapters, the collectivist value orientation that most Japanese people have affects much of what they do.

The Origins of Asian Collectivism

The standard explanation for differences between the individualistic West and the collectivist East is worth considering briefly. This explanation is also worthy of brief consideration because it is used to describe how and why Japan differs to some extent from her Asian neighbors.

At base, the explanation may seem simplistic, perhaps even absurd, because it has to do with what people eat, what people in the West versus in the East have most depended on for survival over the centuries.[2] It is not, however, the nutrients or even chemicals in this food, but rather, how the food must be produced. In contrast to the cultivation of cereal crops such as wheat in Western civilizations, a long history of wet rice cultivation has helped establish a collectivist value orientation across Asia. Wet rice cultivation is labor intensive and requires group cooperation in community projects to get the water in and out of the field at the right time during the growing seasons. Thus, out of necessity, values favoring more group unity and control over the individual developed through the many centuries of dependence on wet rice cultivation for food. And for Japan in particular, so important is rice to life that much of the culture has been touched by rice in symbolic ways (Ohnuki-Tierney 1993).

Not all Asian societies, however, have equally developed this collectivist value orientation. Most important for our subject, Japan did not develop this collectivist value orientation to the same degree or in the same way as countries such as China. The explanation for this is again related to geography and agriculture: because of the far greater abundance of water coming down from mountains in Japan, wet rice farming did not require such large group projects or large groups working together as in China. Thus, Japan came to have values favoring groups, but relatively small and more independent groups compared to many other Asian nations. In addition, Japan did not have the early development of a strong overarching state to organize irrigation projects that resulted in powerful political elites and dominating state structure as in China (Wittfogel 1957). These "hydraulic empires," as found in early Chinese history, are also said to have led to more rigid social stratification and a powerful political elite able to block changes that were needed for industrialization.

Most important, this meant blocking the emergence of a merchant class with the wealth and influence to threaten political elites favored by the old agricultural economy. As we have already seen, Japan had state-controlled stability and unity only briefly during the Tokugawa shogun, and this fell quickly when Japan was forced to open by the United States in 1853. The rapid changes that followed during the Meiji Restoration (1868) would not have been possible if Japan had the rigid state that in some ways still exists in China.

ASPECTS OF JAPANESE SOCIAL STRUCTURE AND VALUES

Sociologists divide groups into two basic types: **primary groups** are those to which the individual is more strongly attached, where emotional ties are greater, more time is spent with other group members, and a diverse set of personal needs are met. **Secondary groups,** on the other hand, are more temporary; there is less time spent with others in the group, emotional ties between members are less, and the group primarily exists for some specific tasks. The best examples of the first are families and close friendship groups; the best example of the second is a work group.

Sociologists of the nineteenth century concerned with the effects of industrialization discovered that people were coming to attach themselves more often to secondary groups, while primary groups were becoming fewer and weaker. The Western individualistic orientation is no doubt both a cause and an effect of this change in the nature of groups in these societies.

By contrast, in Japan, even industrialized Japan of our day, primary groups remain comparatively more important. More precisely, we can say there remains less distinction between primary groups and what would in some other societies be considered secondary groups at work. Although it is certainly an overstatement to call the Japanese corporation an "extended clan" or family, the tendency for Japanese groups to remain primary groups with respect to many characteristics means that people usually have stronger attachments and loyalty to and even make more self-sacrifice for the work group than is found in the United States.

Extensive research by Lincoln and Kalleberg (1990) indicates that Japanese workers have more satisfaction with their jobs, and even feel more freedom, when working alongside others compared to Americans. Japanese workers are also much more likely to say that they should sacrifice for their work group and that they had more trust and confidence in their co-workers.

Personal Ties and Vertical Groups

The above implies that personal ties between group members are stronger in Japan. But there is another dimension of these group ties that is important in understanding Japan: vertical ties are said to be more extensive than in other industrialized nations, particularly links between superiors and subordinates (Nakane 1970). Most notable is the bonding of pairs of junior and senior partners called the *kōhai-sempai* relationship. Horizontal links between people of equal rank in the group certainly exist, but in contrast to what happens in Western industrial nations, these horizontal relationships are less likely to bring people together. A result of this, we will see, is that vertically based conflicts within groups are comparatively rare in Japan, but horizontally based conflicts are not so rare.

Critiques of this view charge that Japanese people socialize no less with co-workers of equal rank than in other countries, that there is identification with the common interests of co-workers, and that the worker versus manager line of conflict is as likely in Japan as elsewhere (Mouer and Sugimoto 1986). It seems, however, that most of the controversy has stemmed from an overemphasis on the vertical nature of the Japanese group: vertical groups are relatively more important in Japan, but horizontal ties certainly do exist, even if in somewhat weaker form. There is increasing evidence for this statement; again we can turn to Lincoln and Kalleberg's (1990) study for empirical support. The Japanese in this study had more frequent interactions with superiors and less with equal co-workers compared to Americans, were more likely to prefer help and advice from superiors, and were more likely to say their boss was involved in many aspects of their lives and to say they liked it this way. In contrast, most Americans said their jobs were more rewarding when their boss left them alone and they preferred to interact much more with equal co-workers than do Japanese.

In some cases, formal ranking is accepted by Japanese as a kind of fiction. Many smaller companies of a few hundred employees have company presidents who have been hired as figureheads after retirement from a large corporation. Their former status can sometimes help a smaller company gain response from bureaucrats, but the figurehead presidents usually have no power within the company at all, with the actual authority residing with the real owner who calls himself vice president or director. Some company presidents may not even visit the company frequently or know anything at all about the business. Every clerk in the office is totally aware of the meaninglessness of the president's rank and of where the power actually resides, but any time those same clerks encounter the president, they will show every bit as much formal deference as if he were in fact in charge. There is not the slightest feeling of deviousness in this kind of situation in Japan. The Japanese honor ranking for its own sake and tend not to analyze what it actually means in terms of power.

Role Playing and Interaction Rituals

There is even a name given to this sort of practice. It is called *tatemae,* "the official version," or "the facade" of a situation. The reality behind the facade is referred to as *honne,* "the way things actually are." Japanese people learn to put up what we might call "a false front" and provide other people what can be inaccurate descriptions or explanations of a situation when they believe the situation or obligation to their group or superiors requires them to do so. And rather than being seen as having a character flaw, the person presenting the false front may be evaluated quite positively for doing so, even by those Japanese people being given the inaccurate information. Japanese people are likely to agree that such behavior is honorable when done to protect one's group or superior.

One of America's most respected sociologists, Erving Goffman (1959, 1963, 1967), developed a perspective often called **dramaturgical theory,** which suggests all human interaction can be compared to roles played in stage dramas. In other words, Goffman took quite literally the lines from Shakespeare's *As You Like It,* which begins, "All the world's a stage, And all men and women merely players." Some key concepts in this dramaturgical theory are *role performance* and *impression management;* the latter term is used to suggest that the person is competent in the role he or she is playing at the time, be it father, mother, professor, student athlete, student leader, playboy, or whatever. Some have charged that Goffman had a rather cynical view of human behavior because his theory suggests people are simply trying to manipulate others by giving such performances (Gouldner 1973). Others, however, argue there are "sincere performances" and "insincere performances," and of course from the Western, especially American, perspective, an insincere performance is to be condemned.

With the example of interaction ritual and Goffman's dramaturgical theory and its criticisms, however, we can understand another difference between Japanese and American value orientations. We can say that tatemae is the essence of an insincere performance and that Japanese people are taught to play them well. A Japanese person can be highly respected when giving such an insincere performance in the proper context. To use a common example, a typical complaint of Westerners working with Japanese people is that "they always say yes even when they mean no." What these Westerners do not fully understand is that Japanese people do not like direct confrontations or conflict, and a simple yes when they actually mean no can avoid this. Other Japanese who understand the concepts of tatemae and honne can distinguish cues in the interaction ritual that let them know which one the other person is presenting. They are likely to know, for example, that they are being told yes but no is meant, and they respect the person for really saying no in a tatemae and, therefore, in a polite manner. Westerners not knowing these Japanese customs miss the whole point and perhaps feel they have been deceived.

Conformity

It is quite likely that more inaccuracies have been written about "conformity," "obedience," and "lack of conflict" in Japan than about any other subject. Pressure to conform in Japan is great; but the pressure to conform is not as highly successful as usually thought in the West, nor does the conformity that does exist come easily, naturally, or without unhappiness for Japanese people. This, in fact, is the real stuff of classic Japanese novels from the Meiji period through the turn of the century to today. Most of the characters in the great novels of Soseki, for example, are rebels—they defy authorities, face inner conflict, and struggle against the pressure to conform.[3] But the pressure to conform in Japan is great, and in the end it is rather more successful than in countries like the United States.

In contrast to the Western proverb that "the squeaky wheel gets the grease," the commonly heard Japanese saying is "the nail that sticks out gets pounded down." Again, the point is that the pressure to conform is great; it produces inner conflict, at times individual trauma, and is often resisted, otherwise so much effort to try to enforce conformity would be unnecessary.

Group Conflict

Now for the other subject in this set: Contrary to the impressions of most people today, Japanese history has been full of conflict. We do not mean only the conflict of samurai armies, with one feudal lord against another or against the shogun. No, peasants have rebelled, workers have rebelled, students have rebelled, and the list can go on and on.[4] With respect to strikes and labor protest, from the 1970s to the present, Japan has recorded some of the lowest rates in the world; but a look through Japanese history, and especially since the 1860s, shows the present to be rather atypical.

In addition to the unacknowledged but humanly normal psychological tension resulting from attempts to assure obedience in Japan, it is the group nature of the Japanese society and culture that misleads people about conflict in Japan. It is often assumed that in a society in which group attachments are very strong there will be little conflict. Actually, and especially in the case of Japan, the opposite can in fact be the case. Classic and contemporary social science theory and research shows that a strong sense of "in-group" almost certainly produces an equally strong sense of "out-group."[5] And also likely with a strong sense of in-group is conflict with the out-group. The main question, as we will see, concerns where to draw the lines between the in-group and out-group. Often this line is drawn between the Japanese and people of other nations. At times it is between one corporation and another, say Toyota versus Nissan. And at other times it can be one family clan versus another, or students versus police, and so on. It is for this reason also that old conflicts seem to go on for longer, with dedicated in-group members loyally keeping up the conflict in the name of the group when the reasons for the conflict seem to have disappeared long ago (as the student rebels who have not stopped their battle against the Narita Airport for over 20 years since it has opened!).

Social Control of Individual Behavior

Differences in the way societies control the behavior of their members are rather subtle, things anthropologists and sociologists notice after long and careful observation. The way people actually behave on a day-to-day basis doesn't actually vary much in practical terms from society to society. Most people follow the rules of proper behavior most of the time, but under the right circumstances, many will lie and cheat when it benefits their best interests. In this regard,27 the Japanese are no different than any other people. What we describe below is not so much a difference in conformity as a difference in the route taken to achieve conformity to norms.

There is a tendency in Western societies to conceive of morality in terms of broad abstractions of *good* and *evil*. Western societies have had a long experience with monotheism, and traditionally in those societies ethics and morality have been interpreted as coming from religion, or perhaps more specifically, from the commandments of an all-powerful God. Except for the tiny minority of Christian and Moslem Japanese, people in that society have never worshiped a monotheistic God. In fact, there is not even a very good word for God in the Japanese language. Beginning around 1920, Japanese translators began using the term *kamisama* to render the Western concept of God into Japanese, taken from *kami*, which traditionally referred both to the many demigods in Japanese polytheism and to a kind of supernatural force inherent in various elements of nature. The point is that throughout history, morality and ethics have not in Japan ever emanated from God or in any other way from religion. Ethics and morality in Japan are not universalistic; rather, they are based more on specific obligations to people and institutions.

Western religions are full of universal concepts. The Ten Commandments, for example, are presumably meant to apply to all situations in life. People in Western societies, whether religious or not, have been taught to see standards of behavior in that kind of universalistic perspective. The Japanese do not have a strongly developed sense of universal good or evil. They do have an extremely well-developed sense of personal obligation. This is not obligation to a set of principles, but *obligation to specific people and organizations* (Benedict 1947).

In understanding the historical context of morality in the West, one must be familiar with the concept of *sin*. There is no exact translation for the word *sin* in Japanese, but two words are equally important in understanding the historical context of Japanese morality. They are *giri* and *on*. They mean roughly the same thing, and in contemporary usage they are often treated as synonyms. Both terms are commonly translated into English as "obligation." To explain the differences, we can say that *giri* is "achieved" obligation, and *on* is "ascribed" obligation. *Giri* traditionally has carried with it the meaning of obligation acquired through some act of help (or kindness or mercy) received from someone who was not obligated to give it. In other words, *giri* is the feeling of debt one owes to another for a significant, albeit unnecessary, favor. *Giri* of course must be repaid, and the favor must be returned with at least as significant a reward as received. The longer one waits to repay *giri*, the deeper it gets, and so the reward should be increased accordingly. Japanese people feel that extremely deep *giri* can never be paid off, that one must sort of pay on the interest throughout life, meaning that the person will be in someone's debt forever and owe them certain kinds of smaller favors from time to time.

On tends to refer to obligation owed to someone or something just because it is there, a factor of support, protection, or nurture built into one's life and to which one should feel gratitude. For example, people owe *on* to their parents. The Chinese character meaning "teacher" is pronounced *shi* in Japanese, and people in Japan often refer to a favorite or particularly helpful teacher or professor as their *onshi*. Before the end of World War II, all Japanese were taught that they owed *on* to the emperor, a way of emphasizing commitment to the nation that was particularly effective in terms of Japanese culture.

There is less a tendency in Japan to think of something as inherently good or bad, and conversely more of a tendency to evaluate behavior as to how it affects others within one's social network. Some writers call this tendency "situational ethics," and the label often has a negative interpretation in the U.S. and other Western societies, described as a kind of creeping moral sloppiness that deviates from timeless standards of right and wrong. But in Japan it definitely does not represent any type of "creeping." The Japanese have throughout history interpreted moral behavior more in terms of obligations, and of course obligations depend on one's social relationships at the time—in other words, on the situation.

Although the mechanisms of behavior control might not always make sense to outsiders, no one could deny that it works. Japan has remarkably high standards of ethical behavior in the context of a large, complex society full of anonymity. Every foreigner who has ever lived in Japan for any length of time can relate stories of valuable items left out in public places, which were still there when the owner returned hours later to look for them. Japanese retailers have a hard time with space, and retailers such as drugstores normally stock items for sale during hours of operation around corners on the outside of the store, completely out of sight of store personnel. Virtually no merchandise ever turns up missing. Can you imagine what would happen if a store tried that in the United States?

Inside/Outside

In Japan, in many interesting ways, there is an unusually strong sense of *inside* and *outside*. Social boundaries in Japan tend to be very starkly drawn. You will see when you read Chapter 11 that in Japan there is a keen awareness of just who is and who is not Japanese, even among families that are not originally Japanese but have resided in Japan for several generations. One can become an American, but it is almost impossible for a non-Japanese to ever assume the identity of Japanese. This is part of a strong inside/outside consciousness, but it goes further than national identity, extending into every facet of life, even to such things as personal residences.

Japanese do most of their socializing outside the home. Normally only relatives and the most intimate of friends ever see the inside of a person's residence unit. Traditional Japanese houses have an entrance alcove called *genkan* that is at ground level below the rest of the house. This is as far as most salespeople, neighbors, and other non-intimate outsiders get when visiting a Japanese home. Inside the home is for people on the "inside." All others are outsiders and are kept outside. In personal relationships, that same strong sense of inside and outside prevails. The organizations a person is associated with—hobby groups, informal groups of close friends, people who have gone to the same schools, and of course work groups—form networks of belongingness that to the Japanese is their social inside.

As you will discover in Chapter 9, students at a Japanese university are not under pressure to study very hard to remain as students at their universities. In fact, some students do not study at all, and still they are virtually guaranteed of graduation after four years of university attendance. If you understand the way concepts of inside and outside work in Japan, the principle of passing students through makes more sense. Students at a university have passed the entrance examination and thereby have become associated with the university. Students there *belong* to the university; they are part of the inside world of the institution. Some day you may refer to a university as your alma mater, but frankly when you use that term, it will simply refer to a place where you went to college. When Japanese use a similar term, *bokō*, "mother school," it has a far deeper meaning, a meaning perhaps only Princeton, Yale, and Harvard graduates could begin to appreciate in this country. It is a place they will identify with in the deepest personal manner all the days of their lives.

Conversely, as part of its own special "inside" for everyone associated with that university, the institution could never treat its students in a cavalier way. The students belong to the institution, it is truly their mother school and will always be, and like a mother, the university is there to help them, not give them a hard time. It will almost guarantee their graduation (regardless of study habits or lack thereof) and it will use all the resources at its command to help the students secure employment after graduation.

CONCLUSION

There has been a tendency for Westerners and even Japanese themselves to believe that Japan is a radically different society when compared to the industrialized nations of Europe and North America. In fact, there is a billion-dollar publishing industry in Japan developed around books popularly called *Nihonjinron,* which means the study of the Japanese. Many of these books make wild claims: Japanese brains are different; Japanese stomachs will not allow them to eat very much Western food because it makes Japanese people different; and on and on. People must be very careful not to assume the Japanese society is so drastically different from those in the West. There are far more similarities than differences.

In this chapter, however, we have tried to note some of the important differences between the Japanese society and Western societies, especially the United States. Being aware of these differences—such things as Japanese collectivism, their greater sense of insider versus outsider, and their sense of obligation to others—will help us to better understand some of the basic subjects that follow in this book.

CHAPTER 3

The Japanese Political System

Throughout history Japan has often had an image problem in the West. Not many years ago, on returning from Japan, we can remember American college students asking if Japan has big buildings and elevators as in the United States. It was probably Godzilla, more than anything else, that finally made people aware of Japan's status as a major industrial power. How else in these old movies could there be all of those buildings for Godzilla to crush? Today, even traveling through the jungles of Southeast Asia or the plains of central Africa it is difficult to miss the fact that Japan is a major industrial power— the automobiles and other manufactured goods encountered are more likely than not from Japan. With relatively cheap seats on Boeing 747s flying in and out of Japan many times a day, the average person is far more likely to have visited Japan than ever before. Still, even when visiting Japan, in some ways the outward signs of Western-style capitalism and democracy can be misleading. Looking more closely at Japan's political-economic system, we find some interesting and, quite often, puzzling differences.

With the economic stagnation Japan has found herself in since the early 1990s, there have been calls for major reforms in the economy and political system. In essence, these calls are for Japan to become more like the United States in major respects—less government regulation in general, and particularly for corporations; a smaller government with fewer government bureaucrats; more free-dom for Japanese corporations to lay off personnel or reduce wages; the list goes on. It is very unlikely much of this will happen, and even less likely that the Japanese government and economy will look much like those in the United States in the future.

In this chapter and the next we will examine the Japanese polit-ical system and economy. In this chapter, we will first consider the Asian concept of power, which can differ from the Western concep-tion, then look at recent Japanese history with respect to political insti-tutions, the Japanese political system today, the great importance and power of government bureaucratic ministers, and finally the peculiar status of the Japanese military today.

POLITICS IN JAPAN

Japan today has a modern and relatively democratic political system. We say "relative" because there are certainly degrees of democracy; the Japanese political system is in some ways less democratic than most Western democratic societies.

Japan has an elected parliament (called a *Diet*) with two sepa-rate houses, much like the British Parliament. The larger and more powerful house of the Diet, with 500 members elected, is called the *lower house* because in the old British system it was made up of the "common people"; the *upper house* was reserved for those with aris-tocratic lineage. Before World War II, in fact, this was still the case in Japan. Today, however, with power in the hands of elected common people in Japan as in England, the lower house has more influence over what government does and which laws are passed.

Elections do have meaning, and the Japanese people do vote politicians out of office from time to time. In some ways Japanese peo-ple have more political democracy than in the United States. For a start, a much greater percentage of the population actually bothers to vote (usually 70 to 80 percent versus the 50 percent or less in the United States); and the very loud sound of trucks moving through the streets of Tokyo all day around election times, blasting out political slogans and the names of politicians seeking votes, gives one the feel-ing that elections are quite important in Japan. As we will see, how-ever, there is an interesting mix of differences and similarities in the Japanese political system.

The Asian Concept of Power

To understand the nature of Japanese politics, we must at least briefly consider another element of Asian culture. The concept of **power**, according to some political scientists such as Lucian Pye (1985), is shaped by cultural definitions. An old element of Asian culture is the ideal of a benevolent, paternalistic leader and the acceptance of dependency for those below the elites. Thus, ancient traditions and Asian religions have shaped a relationship of obligation, duties, responsibilities, and mutual protection between leaders and followers.

In addition to all of this, according to Pye, power through most of Asian history has been a dimension of status or honor, something to be attained as a badge of respect rather than for other purposes, such as to promote specific policy goals, attain more wealth, or control people per se. Power in Asia, in other words, had been something to attain in its own right, simply for the status of having it, rather than for other utilitarian goals. It is here, however, where Japan is said to differ from many of her Asian neighbors. The concept of power in Japan has historically carried a more utilitarian component: it is to be used for something other than just the status of having it, therefore creating objective criteria of success by which to judge leaders (Pye 1985). This is also to say that in Japan there are cultural traditions and old forms of social organization that can help promote democracy with the coming of a modern industrial economy and an educated middle class. It is understandable, then, that Japan had the first functional democratic political system in Asia.

RECENT JAPANESE POLITICAL HISTORY

Not long ago in Japan, even the pretense of democracy did not exist. We must remember that Japan was still a rather traditional feudal country less than 150 years ago and has had a quasi-democratic political system for only some 50 years. Max Weber's (1946) ideal type of **traditional authority** fits the pre-Meiji era, or feudal Japan, rather well. The ruling elite was given legitimacy through a "holy" king (in this case the Japanese emperor), but it was military power that kept the system together when elite rule was threatened. More than in most European varieties of traditional authority during feudalism, however, the Japanese emperor had little real power, which was in fact held by a military clan ruling in the name of the emperor—the famous shogun military clans.

When, in 1853, U.S. gunboats brought Japan back into the international world after more than 200 years, one major section of the samurai political elite soon realized Japan had to change quickly. It was as if they had moved ahead in history to read Skocpol's (1979) account of why revolutions come to political economies forced to compete with nations having more modern and efficient state structures. This educated faction of the samurai in the 1850s saw China, Korea, and most of Southeast Asia already colonized, or in the process of becoming colonies of the Western powers. It was clear that Japan had to modernize rapidly or face the same fate. By 1868, as we have seen, one samurai group staged a military coup to overthrow the last Tokugawa shogun government, then modernize government functions and help bring about rapid economic development. Thus, although their primary aim was economic growth, they soon decided that an outward image of democracy would also be helpful. That the first elected government in Japan at the time was mostly a symbol of the modernization they were seeking is suggested by the first fierce debates over whether or not new Diet members should be allowed inside the Diet without Western-style clothing.

By 1889, a constitution was put in place creating this image of democracy (Gluck 1985). It was written primarily by Hirobumi Ito, who had visited England in the 1880s and was told by the sociologist and social Darwinist Herbert Spencer that Japan should retain "traditional obligations to superiors" (Benedict 1947:81). Whether or not the advice had any effect on Ito, the constitution attempted to do just that.

The new Meiji Constitution was brought in with much ceremony by the emperor, who followed the ritual of going in private to his dead ancestors to tell them of a major change he had proscribed for the people. There were festivals all over Japan for the common people. Days later, Japanese newspapers finally got around to telling people what a constitution and democracy were, though very few understood what it meant even then. Although only 1.1 percent of the people could actually vote under this first constitution (which is actually close to the percentage who could vote in the first years of the Constitution of the United States), the ruling elites were rather worried about political disruptions and challenges to their rule. To prepare the people for the new concept of democracy, the very important "Rescript on Education" was issued under the name of the emperor, which taught the Japanese people of their need to remain loyal to the emperor and nation-state (Gluck 1985). This Rescript came to be a core part of all education in Japan to help legitimize elite rule, that is until the whole system came apart at the end of World War II.

In the roughly 90-year period between the forced opening of Japan (or Meiji Restoration) and the end of World War II, there was some variation in the degree of democracy—from almost none to a slight level of democracy during the short-lived Taisho democracy in the 1920s. But mostly it was a period of very little democracy, which gave fuel to the argument that Asian cultures, especially those with Confucian principles, were unable to establish real democracy. What was happening, however, is best explained by Barrington Moore (1966), who showed how a state forced into the modern era in which it must compete with other modernizing and industrializing nations will turn to something like a fascist dictatorship when neither a capitalist class nor workers or peasants are politically organized. Real democracy can only come when the masses are a political force with which elites must contend.

THE JAPANESE POLITICAL SYSTEM TODAY

With Japan's defeat and the U.S. occupation after World War II, the old Meiji Constitution was thrown out. And in a curious turn of events, after the American occupation forces under General MacArthur rejected attempt after attempt by the Japanese to write a new constitution, MacArthur ordered a small staff of rather inexperienced Americans to write the new constitution for the Japanese, in English, which was then forced upon Japanese politicians (Gibney 1992, 1995). This is the constitution Japan has to this day (Kishimoto 1988), which still in places has awkward phrases in Japanese because it was written originally in English.

Under this postwar constitution there are two houses of the Diet (parliament), much like the British Government, and an independent judicial system. The lower house has many more members (500 in the lower house versus 252 in the upper house) and is much more important than the upper house, which only with great difficulty can block legislation. And while the Japanese emperor has had little power for hundreds of years (being only a figurehead under the shoguns of old), he has no formal power at all today, much like the British queen or king.

Like in the standard parliamentary system of government found all over Europe, the Japanese prime minister is elected by the members of the bigger lower house of parliament. This means that the political party with most members elected to the Diet, until very recently the Liberal Democratic Party in Japan, can elect the prime minister. If one political party does not have a majority of the members of parliament, it must form coalitions with smaller parties to get enough members to "form a government," which is to say elect a prime minister who can then select the cabinet ministers to head the major agencies of government. When it is necessary, as it usually is around the world and even now in Japan, the process of forming a coalition government is slow and complex. Many little parties can be given special benefits if they will support the major party, but the same offerings are likely from the next largest party in parliament, which is also trying to form a coalition government. It is in this sense that a parliamentary system with multiple political parties can sometimes give small political parties representing minority interests in the society political influence they would never have in the two-party American political system.

In Japan, all lower-house members must run for reelection every four years, or sooner if the prime minister is forced to call new elections; whereas all upper-house members must run for reelection every six years, with half the members up for reelection every three years. Under Japan's new election laws that went into effect for the first time during the 1996 general election for the lower house of the Diet, politicians compete for 300 district seats and 200 national proportional seats. The proportional seats are given to candidates of the parties in terms of what percentages of the national vote the parties receive. After the last election in October 1996, of the new 500 seats in the lower house of the Diet, the Liberal Democratic Party had 239, New Frontier had 156, Democrats 52, Social Democrats 15, and Communists 26. Thus, the Liberal Democratic Party again lacked a majority of the seats and had to go back to its coalition government with the Social Democrats.

In one of the most important contrasts to the U.S. political system, and to some extent the British as well, Japan has a much more centralized system of government. There are prefecture (state) governments and other local governments, but they have much less power than state and local governments in the United States—Japan's is certainly not a federal system of government. Whether good or bad, and no doubt there is some of both, this allows the Japanese government to have more coordinated activities and planning, which are lacking in the United States. Finally, despite the centralized nature of the government, we should note that today's Japanese Constitution, in fact, contains more freedoms and provisions to promote democracy than most Western democratic constitutions (Pempel 1989). It includes most of the individual rights and freedoms found in the U.S. Constitution (owning guns is not one of them, however) and even an equal rights amendment for women not found in the United States. As we will see, however, not all of these individual rights are vigorously enforced.

Local Government and Citizen Participation

Although the central Japanese government located in Tokyo is much more powerful than local governments when compared to the United States and most European governments, Japan's local governments are of course still important. Much of the actual management of problems on the local level is done by local government offices; things such as roads, bridges, and school buildings must be built and social workers managed by local governments. There are 47 prefectures in Japan (like U.S. states), which have their own governments and are headed by the equivalent of an American state governor elected by the people of the prefecture. There are also 200 city governments in Japan, with city councils and mayors as in the United States.

There are, however, some big differences when these local governments are compared to those in the United States. As already noted, they have much less power and independence. Most of what these local politicians can and cannot do is determined by the national government in Tokyo. For example, these local governments can hire teachers, but what is taught is regulated by the Ministry of Education in Tokyo. Also, the courts and police are run by the national government. The most important limitation to local government influence, however, comes from the control of government money by the central government in Tokyo. The vast majority of taxes collected in Japan are collected by the central government, and the money needed to run public schools, build bridges in local areas, along with almost everything else, is given to the local governments by the national government. If the central government does not like what is being done in local areas, it cuts off the money.

There is increasing reaction against so much power in the hands of the central government. Citizen protest movements are taking place all over Japan on many issues. All 200 towns in Japan and all but one prefecture (46 of 47) have passed disclosure laws so that citizens can have more information about exactly what government is doing. Citizen ombudsman groups that represent and look after the interests of common citizens are becoming popular. But there are many loopholes in the laws, and the federal courts have not ruled in favor of any of these important demands as yet. For many decades to come, the central government in Japan will continue to hold much more power than the central governments of other advanced industrialized nations.

Special Interests and Money Politics

There are other common limits to democracy in Japan, however. Perhaps even more than in most democratic societies today, it takes money to get elected and reelected in Japan—lots of money. It can be said that money has corrupted democracy in Japan more than in any other major industrial nation, with the possible exception of Italy (Woronoff 1986; Curtis 1988; Kishimoto 1988). Officially the Communist Party in Japan takes in the largest amount of money for campaigning, though all agree these figures are grossly inaccurate. Between 1955 and 1993, one political party, the Liberal Democratic Party (LDP), ruled the Diet, and some 90 percent of LDP campaign funds came from large corporations.

A result of all this is that election to the Diet can bring money— again, lots of it. Although Japanese politicians are legally paid only about $160,000 per year, they can end up being very rich. A revealing survey of the wealth of Diet members, required for the first time by a law that went into effect in 1993, provided a rough estimate of their assets (*Japan Times International Weekly*, June 21, 1993). The 1992 assets of the 749 Diet members, including both upper and lower houses, averaged $843,800 per member. For LDP members alone the average was $1.25 million per member, with LDP politicians accounting for three-quarters of all assets of Diet members and 87 of the richest members.

Still, politicians do not get in the Diet without enough votes from the people. As a result, when it comes time for national elections, most voters in Japan have been conditioned to think of what politicians can do for their local needs. Herein comes the root of what Americans call "pork-barrel" politics—politicians are rated by how many bridges, roads, libraries, civic centers, and so forth have been forthcoming, not on ideology nor on pressing national or world issues. In addition, powerful politicians are not much affected by their involvement in scandals: Tanaka, Takeshita, and all of the others were reelected again and again even after being implicated in financial scandals, because they could deliver the goods to local voters.

THE MINISTRY BUREAUCRATS

There is, however, a much greater limitation to government democracy in Japan than those described above. A political cartoon we saw recently (and, we might add, before the April 1995 gas attack by the Aum Shinrikyō religious cult) suggests the situation: Two policemen are seen standing across the street from the Diet building in front of another building most Japanese recognize as the Diet members' office quarters. Scurrying in the background are what appear to be civil disaster workers carrying stretchers with bodies on them. One policeman says, "What a tragedy that the gas leak caused all the Diet members to be found dead at their desks." The other policeman adds, "Yes, but great luck that the gas leak was confined to this one building so that no important functions of government are directly affected."

With the centralized nature of the Japanese government, one can begin to understand the overwhelming power of unelected ministry bureaucrats in the Japanese political system. These are the people implied in the cartoon who were not in the building, who do serve very important government functions. The cartoon is a little exaggerated, but much of what is done by government in Japan is done by these unelected officials, who have few restraints over them from the elected side of government. These people are career civil servants who have started their jobs soon after college graduation and worked their way into top ministry positions by their 50s, and sometimes earlier.

Another set of numbers indicates the power of these Japanese ministry bureaucrats. When a new president of the United States takes office, that person can appoint over 2,000 top government bureaucratic officials, all answerable to the president. When a new Japanese prime minister takes office, he/she can appoint only 20 such people; the others are already in place in the form of career ministry bureaucrats who cannot be hired or fired by the prime minister. Even more important, in another big contrast to the United States, Japanese politicians lack sufficient staff to gather information and write legislation, and in most cases they have far less knowledge and experience about important issues than the ministry elite. Most legislation that passes the Diet every year is written by, and promoted by, these unelected ministry officials. Further, the way these laws are written gives ministry bureaucrats extensive leeway in interpreting them through "administrative guidance." And in any case, the ministry officials issue ordinances that outnumber laws passed in the Diet by 9 to 1 (Koh 1989).

There are what can be seen as positive and negative points of this Japanese system of government. Some of the negative points are increasingly debated in Japan today, such as inflexible government rules that hamper business competitiveness. Of course, it's very difficult for the Japanese people to have much influence on what their government does when these unelected bureaucratic officials have such power. Given the political rhetoric in Japan, especially during election times, it may seem similar as to what occurs in the United States, but one must realize the Japanese system has many, many more rules and regulations than the American system ever had.

Among the positive points of the Japanese political system is that it has allowed for much more coordination of the economy, economic planning, and long-term planning to deal with many types of social problems (Johnson 1982; Kerbo and McKinstry 1995). In Chapter 4, we will consider the economic coordinating function of government in more detail and examine the Japanese economy today.

THE JAPANESE MILITARY

The final arm of government we will consider in this chapter is one of the most common and important elements of a modern government: the military. One of the primary legitimate functions of national governments around the world is to maintain some type of force to protect citizens from outside threats. In the case of Japan, however, the military is in a rather unique position. Soon after World War II, as we have seen earlier, the U.S. occupation forces that governed the country imposed a new constitution on Japan. Contained in this is the famous Article 9:

> Aspiring sincerely to an international peace based on justice and order, the Japanese people forever renounce war as a sovereign right of the nation and the threat or use of force as means of settling international disputes.
>
> In order to accomplish the aim of the preceding paragraph, land, sea, and air forces, as well as other war potential, will never be maintained. The right of belligerency of the state will not be recognized.

In essence, Japan could have no military as dictated by the United States. Military restrictions were placed on Germany after World War II, but nothing like what was done in Japan. Soon after the war, the Japanese people supported Article 9. In large part, this support continues today, and most Japanese are quite proud of the country's antiwar stand. In fact, in a national poll within 19 nations asking the people if they would be willing to fight in a war for their country, the United States was number one, with 77 percent saying they would do so; Japan was last, with only 6 percent of the population saying they would do so (Shapiro 1992: 43).

After China fell to the Communists in 1949, after the experiences of the Korean War a couple of years later, and then the Cold War, the U.S. government began to rethink this antimilitary Article 9 forced on Japan. Japan, or at least most of Japan's citizens, on the other hand, rather liked the antiwar stance of their country. Gradually, however, a quasi-legal compromise was worked out so that Japan could have what is called the Self Defense Force (SDF). By informal agreement in the Diet, spending on the military (the SDF) is generally limited to 1 percent of Japan's gross national product, compared to 5 to 7 percent for the United States in the last few decades. Further, all activities of this military force must be defensive in nature. There is to be no military equipment that can be used in an offensive war, which generally implies that no means of transporting military troops and equipment far from Japanese shores is allowed. Through treaties worked out with the U.S. government, Japan is to have only enough personnel and military equipment to protect itself from attack for a few days until the U.S. military can come to help them. This is the primary reason that many U.S. military bases are still located on Japanese soil, though the Japanese pay for 70 percent of the cost of having these U.S. forces in Japan.

It is commonly assumed that America's extensive military spending has harmed the U.S. economy (Thurow 1991), whereas the Japanese are free to spend more of their resources on developing new consumer goods to sell to America. It is for this reason that there has been extensive pressure on Japan from the United States to pay for more of its own military protection. But extensive military development in Japan is not likely to come for many, many decades. Japan's neighbors, such as China and all of the Southeast Asian nations, remember the brutality of Japanese military dominance during World War II, and from even earlier in the case of Taiwan and Korea. Whenever there is even a hint that Japan will expand its military, these governments file diplomatic protests and many of their citizens take to the streets in sometimes violent protest.

CONCLUSION

In this chapter we have considered how the Asian concept of power differs from that of the West, but also how Japan does not follow this concept of power to the same degree as most other Asian nations. We then considered recent Japanese political history and the situation today in Japan. We have seen that special interest groups are very powerful in Japan and that local government plays a much smaller role there than in the United States. Finally, we have considered the place of Japan's very small military, the Self Defense Force, and why the military will remain small in Japan.

The movement of history has shown that totalitarian government in not compatible with advanced industrial economies (Lenski 1966; Lenski, Lenski, and Nolan 1991). The old Chinese elites who follow after the death of Deng Xiaoping in 1997 will eventually have to go if China is to fully modernize and industrialize as they hope. Throughout Asia, increasing democracy has come with economic development in countries such as South Korea, Taiwan, and Thailand, and even Vietnam is likely to follow in coming decades.

This does not mean, however, that democracy will work the same all over the world. The details about how democracy will be implemented and institutionalized will certainly vary. Much of this variation is shaped by the values and traditions of each country. Asian democracy, this is to say, will not be identical to democracy in Western countries such as the United States. In this chapter we have tried to show some of the details of the Japanese political system. Japan does have a democratic political system, and in some ways it seems more democratic than that of the United States. But there are, and will continue to be, differences throughout Asia that must be recognized by anyone trying to understand modern Japan.

CHAPTER 4

The Japanese Economy

As we have seen, Japan developed its industrial economy much more recently than the other industrial nations. Also, Japan was the first Asian country to become an industrial society. There are many key questions related to these two facts, all of which pertain to how Japan's economy may differ from those in the United States and European industrial societies. In this chapter we will first see how the Japanese went about promoting economic development almost 150 years ago and how this resulted in the *zaibatsu* groups of corporate giants. We will then examine how this economic system was changed through U.S. military control after World War II and the subsequent development of the now famous *keiretsu* corporate groups that have made Japan an economic power. Finally, we will look at what it is like to work in Japan today and how that differs from work in the United States.

JAPAN'S ECONOMIC DEVELOPMENT

In 1868, when the rebellious army from the Satsuma and Choshu regions of Japan marched into what is now Tokyo, the revolution, or what was called the Meiji Restoration, had finally come. As we have seen, the primary concern of the new Meiji government was the threat of either European or American colonization and economic exploitation. To prevent this colonization, the new political elites wanted industrialization, and they wanted it fast. As they correctly ascertained, only a powerful economy and military of their own would bring them security and equal treatment with the Western powers.

In effect, a kind of **forced industrialization** and modernization took place, all orchestrated by the new government, which has since been described as a **capitalist development state** (Johnson 1982). As late developing societies (societies developing after the first industrial nations achieved such status), both Germany and Japan have had and continue to have much more government involvement in economic expansion, though Japan's has been more extreme. It has been particularly Japan that has since provided a model of industrialization for many countries undergoing successful economic development today, especially those in Asia (Dietrich 1991; Vogel 1991; Fallows 1994; Kerbo and McKinstry 1995), defying the old economic theories that claim that such state involvement in the economy will not work.

With this capitalist development state, the Japanese first sent many of its best and brightest to Europe during the late 1800s to study the institutions of the West, who later reported back as to what could best work for Japan. (They especially liked and copied many aspects of Bismarck's Germany.) Japan then set about to create a capitalist industrial economy, skipping many stages of the more gradual development that had occurred in the West. And in the process, the new Meiji government also created an **upper class** of wealthy families called the *zaibatsu*, which soon came to almost completely dominate the Japanese economy in the pre–World War II era. These families created many types of corporations, in several industries, which were all linked to the central family stock-holding company and a main bank, as well as linked through various business deals with each other. The biggest of these old zaibatsu include many corporate names well known today, such as Mitsui, Fujita, and Sumitomo (Morikawa 1992).

THE ZAIBATSU

All of the big zaibatsu families, in one way or another, developed and grew in the late 1800s and early 1900s through sponsorship and protection by the political elites (Morikawa 1992). In some cases the government granted them exclusive rights to certain economic activities, as with Mitsui's first role as banker to the new government. In other cases the new government started its own industries, especially when it was judged that these industries were most important for rapid industrialization. Being rather inept in this activity, however, the government-run industries usually did not operate very efficiently and were soon sold to private owners. Few Japanese, of course, had the money or access to government loans for such purchases; but some of the old merchant families had enough money, as did many former daimyo (feudal lords) and samurai who were given government compensation after losing their old positions after 1868. Thus, through extremely low-cost deals on struggling government companies, then more government protection, others became wealthy zaibatsu families.

As a result, before World War II just the top 10 zaibatsu families in Japan controlled about 75 percent of all corporate assets (Halliday 1975: 180; Alletzhauser 1990: 108). There was a rigid class system with little mobility into top positions. Exploitation was extreme. In contrast to today's small income gap between corporate elites and workers (about 17 to 1), the gap before the war was around 100 to 1 (Abegglen and Stalk 1985: 191). Extensive starvation was not uncommon in the prewar countryside, and parents sometimes sold their daughters into prostitution rather than see them starve (Hane 1982). Taxes took about 35 percent of the crop, and rents paid to landowners usually took another 50 percent. There were many peasant revolts and violent urban strikes during the 50 years that preceded World War II, all violently suppressed (Bowen 1980; Hane 1982, 1988; Gluck 1985). In short, Japan was not the country of harmony, relative equality, and cooperation that is often depicted today.

U.S. Occupation Reforms and the Rise of the Keiretsu

Before the end of World War II, the Mitsui family was the richest in Japan, indeed, one of the world's most wealthy. Then, soon after the end of World War II, on October 8, 1945, two trucks under U.S. Army escort pulled up at the Mitsui headquarters in Tokyo. The drivers got out and, with the help of some Mitsui employees, loaded onto the trucks some 42 wooden cases containing $281 million in

Mitsui securities; soon, the securities were gone, and with them the Mitsui zaibatsu that had dominated Japan's prewar economy. In 1947, the new American-backed Japanese government placed an extensive tax on the remaining wealth of the leading zaibatsu families, and then in 1948, the "Law of the Termination of Zaibatsu" took away almost all of the rest (Morikawa 1992: 237): The most wealthy 56 zaibatsu families lost almost everything. For example, the head of the main Mitsui family at the time, Hachiroemon Mitsui, was forced to give up 91 percent of his remaining family wealth. He, along with the rest of the Mitsui clan, was never to dominate a company, let alone the country, again. Hachiroemon Mitsui used some of his remaining money to buy a little schoolhouse where he spent his remaining years running his own small kindergarten. Hachiroemon continued to have some property in Japan, but his total income in 1970 was reported to have been only $28,000 (Roberts 1976: 410).

The new Japanese government, still directed by General MacArthrr, could take such drastic action because (with only some justification) the Japanese people blamed the zaibatsu families for tricking them into a war with the United States. But even though the most wealthy zaibatsu families had their wealth taken away, the interlocked system of corporations they developed soon reemerged (Kerbo and McKinstry 1995). At first the old corporate names were disallowed (names such as Mitsui and Sumitomo), and the managers who used to run these corporations for the zaibatsu families were prohibited from taking up business positions again. But, with growing pressure for rapid reconstruction of Japan following Mao's Communist victory in China, and after the Korean War broke out, such efforts were given up.

THE KEIRETSU TODAY

These interlocked groups of corporations are now called *keiretsu* and resemble the old zaibatsu corporate groups in most ways; the big difference is simply that the family control is gone. At the end of World War II, 70 percent of corporate stock in Japan was family owned. Today about 80 percent of corporate stock is owned by other corporations—that is, the corporations own each other (Dore 1987: 113; Morioka 1989: 155; Kerbo and McKinstry 1995: 65). Studies have found, for example, that among the top 300 corporations in Japan, only

TABLE 4-1

Stock Holdings within the Mitsubishi Keiretsu

The Mitsubishi Group of Interlocked Corporations	
Company of Stock Issue	Percent of Stock Owned Within the Mitsubishi Group
Mitsubishi Bank	26.9%
Mitsubishi Trust Bank	32.3
Tokyo Marine	21.7
Mitsubishi Heavy Industries	23.2
Mitsubishi Corporation	42.2
Mitsubishi Electric	16.3
Asahi Glass	29.3
Kirin Beer	12.7
Mitsubishi Chemical	24.5
N.Y.K. Shipping	27.5

Source: Kerbo and McKinstry (1995), p. 71.

6 percent of the stock is held by individuals or families (Kerbo and Nakao 1991). In one sense it can be said today that Japan is a capitalist society with few true capitalists. The nature of these interlocked keiretsu corporate groups can be seen in Table 4–1, which shows the Mitsubishi keiretsu and the cross-stock-holding among some of the main companies in this keiretsu.

There is wide agreement in Japan on the six most powerful keiretsu today. These corporate groups, called *horizontal keiretsu,* include Mitsubishi, Mitsui, Sumitomo, Fuji, Daiichi Kangyo, and Sanwa (Ōsono 1991; Kerbo and McKinstry 1995). Depending on the definition followed, these big six together contain from 187 to 193 main corporations, accounting for about 15 percent of all corporate assets, including 40 percent of all banking assets, 53 percent of all insurance assets, and 53 percent of the real estate business (Morioka 1989: 49; Ōsono 1991; Gerlach 1992: 87). On the average, each of the 187 to 193 corporations within one of the big six is linked through stock ownership with 54 percent of the other companies within the group, with an average of 21.6 percent of the stock of each of these corporations held collectively by other corporations within the group.

There are actually two types of keiretsu in Japan today, with the other best described as *vertical keiretsu*. At the center of a vertical keiretsu is always a major corporation (a corporation within one of the big six horizontal keiretsu, for example), with smaller companies dependent on the big company as suppliers or providers of other important business resources tied to the central corporation on down the line. This is what forms Japan's **dual economy** (Beck, Horan, and Tolbert 1978; Tolbert, Horan, and Beck 1980). To an even greater extent than in the United States, in fact, Japan's dual economy is divided between large firms with higher profits, more market control, higher wages, and more unionization, and smaller firms having all of these characteristics in much smaller degrees (Clark 1979: 143; Lincoln and Kalleberg 1985, 1990; Kalleberg and Lincoln 1988; Ishida 1993: 224). This aspect of Japan's dual economy also must be kept in mind when we hear stories of workers with lifetime employment in one corporation and extensive worker benefits, such as company housing, in Japanese corporations. These things do exist in Japan, but primarily for the 30 percent of Japanese workers in the core sector of the dual economy, which is to say the big corporations of the horizontal keiretsu.

It is the keiretsu that form the essence of the Japanese economic might today and create several of the key features of the Japanese economy. As we have said before, Japan is a nation of groups, and corporations are no exception. These keiretsu groups of corporations help each other, trade with each other, exchange personnel, and work together as lobby organizations for mutual interests. If one company is in trouble, for example, others in the keiretsu will help it through the rough times (Lincoln, Gerlach, and Takahashi 1992; Lincoln, Gerlach, and Ahmadjian 1996). And these keiretsu executives, especially the presidents' clubs (discussed in Chapter 6), operate to restrain the behavior of other executives in the group. If wage demands of one executive within the keiretsu become excessive, or if performance lags, the others in the keiretsu will act to discipline that person for the good and survival of the whole group—which sometimes does not happen in other capitalist countries such as the United States.

It is important to note that what all of the above also means is that to a much greater extent than in the United States, Japanese executives and board members of the biggest companies are corporate bureaucrats rather than rich capitalists. These Japanese executives are company men, with relatively low incomes, who must worry about their retirement pensions being enough to take care of them when they are too old to work. However, there are some very wealthy people in Japan today. Like Taikichiro Mori who, with $15 billion in assets, recently dropped off the top of the list of most wealthy in the world when he died, these superrich in Japan have most often made their millions or billions through real estate manipulations and are often looked down on as *nari-agari,* "new rich status climbers" (Hamabata 1990: 5). Of the 100 top income earners in Japan in 1991, for example, 85 made their income primarily in real estate speculation. These people, however, are not most important in Japan's corporate economy today, nor are they very powerful.

WORKING IN JAPAN

The Japanese workplace is in the process of change since the downturn of Japan's powerful economy in the first half of the 1990s. Also, there has been much distorted information about Japanese management styles and work in Japan in recent years. As already noted, for example, lifetime employment does exist in Japan, but only for about 30 percent of the employees who work for the biggest corporations in Japan's dual economy.[6] There are, however, some standard features of the Japanese workplace that are in big contrast to working in America.

The information about how many hours Japanese workers put into their jobs is not distorted; they work longer hours than the people of any other major industrial nation.[7] At an average of over 2,000 hours per worker per year, Japan is ahead of them all. Japanese workers commonly work six days a week, for much more than eight hours a day on most days. German workers have the lowest hours worked per year (1,600); the United States is second only to Japan and fast closing in on the 2,000-hour-per-year mark.

Although the number of hours worked each year is coming down in Japan, it is a difficult problem to solve. It is not so much that Japanese workers are forced to work such long hours, but that dedication to the company and co-workers makes Japanese people feel guilty if they do not stay in the office late or give up some of their vacation time. One large Japanese bank, for example, started a policy of requiring lights to be turned off after a certain hour at night one day a week. Many, however, claim the result has been longer hours of work on other days. Another company one of us observed while living in Hiroshima for a year would close all blinds during the holidays so workers could not be seen at work at these times.

The hard work and company devotion in Japan cannot be well understood unless we remember the greater importance of the group in Japan than in the United States. Nor can other aspects of the Japanese workplace be well understood without this focus on the group. For example, one study of the seven leading capitalist nations asked managers if long-term employees should be fired if their performance suddenly went down. The highest response of yes was in the United States at 77 percent, whereas only 33 percent in Japan and 31 percent in Germany responded yes (Hampden-Turner and Trompenaars 1993: 112). In fact, in Japan there is a special "position" and word to describe low-performing workers, but workers companies are unwilling to fire—*madogiwazoku*, or "window person." After the boss and co-workers give up on trying to improve the performance of the person, his or her desk is placed by a window where he or she is left alone. With a long recession in the 1990s and new competition from a revitalized U.S. economy, Japan is slowly changing. For example, some Japanese companies are starting to lay off workers for the first time, and the ones to go first are usually the window people. Still, Japanese companies have a long way to go to be like those in the United States in laying off workers, if they ever get there.

Finally, in this context we can mention the standard Japanese promotion policies that Americans usually find surprising. Although there is some change with this policy in Japan, the typical practice is that all employees are promoted together according to age, not in terms of some special achievement criteria. The first question from Americans is usually, "How can they motivate anyone to work hard if there is no special incentive?" Again, we must remember the importance of the group, in this case work group, in Japan. The Japanese view is that rewarding one person over others can cause conflict. On the other hand, rewarding the group as a whole for achievement creates more unity and improves group performance (Hampden-Turner and Trompenaars 1993: 59). Also, because of the importance of the peer group to Japanese workers, money is less of a motivating factor than judgments of co-workers. Even with no special pay considerations, Japanese workers feel that dedication and hard work are necessary to gain the approval of other group members.

Having said all of this, however, we must note that under some circumstances American-style individualism and interpersonal competition do appear in the career equation of Japanese white-collar employees. Not every person of the same age can be promoted together forever; at the top of the employee ladder, the positions start to become fewer. This is to say, not everyone in the company or government agency can be company president or government vice minister. At around age 55 to 60, only a few are promoted to the top, and those who are not will be forced to retire—in fact, they choose to retire, because it would normally be considered degrading to suddenly have a peer become one's boss. It is here that individual merit and achievement over one's long career finally lead to selection over peers.

Worker Influence and Unions

Corporate bureaucracies in Japan are noted for having more ranks and levels than most others (Lincoln and Kalleberg 1990; Gerlach 1992). But it is also interesting that there tend to be fewer observable rank distinctions in Japanese corporations (Clark 1979: 215), even in overseas operations of Japanese corporations with foreign employees (Kerbo, Wittenhagen, and Nakao 1994; Lincoln, Kerbo, and Wittenhagen 1995; Kerbo and Slagter 1996). In many ways, higher management is not treated so differently: managers eat in the same places as workers; they do not have large and separate offices or executive washrooms.

None of this, however, suggests that workers are equal and find no need for unions. In most respects, it can be said that labor unions in Japan are weaker than in Europe, though stronger than in the United States in recent years (Woodiwiss, 1990; Kerbo and McKinstry 1995: Chap. 9). This statement, however, must be qualified. The first thing to note is that many unions in Japan are company unions, in contrast to, say, the United Auto Workers in the United States, which represents workers across many companies. There are nationwide union coalitions in Japan, with *Ringo* the most powerful. These are the unions responsible for what is traditionally called *shunto*, the "spring wage offensive," which have been rather successful in obtaining contracts with higher wages each year. Union coalitions, in effect, coordinate their demands to try to achieve more strength in this annual negotiation process.

In the U.S. experience, a "company union" usually implies that the union is controlled by the company and has no real power. This sometimes is the case in Japan, because the Japanese idea of worker-management conflict is different. Thus, the Japanese more often see teamwork rather than an adversary relationship existing in worker-management situations. This may in large part be corporate ideology at work, but the unions in Japan in many cases push management rather hard in protecting their interests (Dore 1987).

Another aspect of corporate bureaucracy is the extent to which workers have some influence or say in what happens in the workplace. It is commonly believed that, with quality control circles and other management techniques used in Japan, there is intensive group decision making and that workers have much say in how their jobs are done. Not everyone agrees with this theory (Nakane 1970; Woronoff 1980; Price 1997), but it can give workers the impression of collective decision making, thereby making them feel more important. This may also make them feel more responsible for the decision if something goes wrong and more cooperative in trying to correct mistakes.

CONCLUSION

In this chapter we have described how the Japanese economy developed soon after the country opened up and the Meiji Restoration (1868) occurred. From this beginning, Japan was a capitalist state that was very active in promoting development. We explained the early zaibatsu structure of corporations and how these developed into what are the important keiretsu corporate structures. Finally, we considered the nature of work in Japan and the place of labor unions.

In the past, Western economists have tended to assume there are "valueless" or "value neutral" capitalist systems. They now make that assumption at the peril of being very wrong (Hofstede 1991). Much the same can be said for democratic political systems. Although there are more similarities than differences between the political and economic systems in Japan and the United States, there are certainly differences. In this chapter we have tried to introduce to you some of the key similarities and differences.

Finally, it is again worth noting that the twenty-first century will be one of economic competition between the great powers. There will no doubt be wars of various types, but not between the major economic powers. This is to say, we take a very negative view of the recent popular book, *The Coming War with Japan* (Friedman and Lebard 1991). Rather, the twenty-first century will be a century of economic conflict, with the winning countries having the most fit economic characteristics and government to support the fit economy. Certainly the three largest industrial powers—the United States, Japan, and Germany—have many important differences in political systems and economies, which make the coming economic competition interesting for social scientists and very serious business for the people of these countries (Thurow 1991).

CHAPTER 5

Social Stratification in Japan

Social stratification, or the system of ranking within a society, is one of the most important topics in sociology. Research has shown that a society's system of social stratification affects such things as people's health, psychological well-being, even their sexual habits, and certainly how much they have of things like money, job security, and education. On the national level, the type of stratification system a country has affects such things a s the level of crime, political stability, and economic performance.

It is important to understand that there are significant differences among stratification systems around the world today. Americans, for example, tend to think that the high degree of income inequality and poverty found in the United States is natural, even inevitable. "The poor you will always have with you" is often the attitude. But even though there may always be poor people, we need to ask how many and how far below others in the society they may be.

In many ways the systems of social stratification in Japan and the United States are quite different. How they are different and what this means for Japan is the general topic of this chapter. In beginning this chapter, we will first note some of the differences between Japan and the United States. We will then consider the nature of class, status, and power divisions in Japan and why Japan has so much less material inequalities than the United States. Finally, we will examine gender and ethnic inequalities and the level of social mobility in Japan (the movement up or down the stratification system among individuals).

SOME CONTRASTS TO THE UNITED STATES

Modern Japan presents something of a puzzle with respect to social stratification, especially when compared to the United States. On the one hand, Japan has one of the most equal income distributions of modern societies. For example, a 1991 survey of annual incomes of top executives in the biggest 838 corporations in Japan found an average of about $378,000, compared to an average of $1.2 million in the United States (and one must keep in mind the higher cost of living in Japan). More generally, several studies have indicated that the income ratio between corporate presidents and average workers in Japan is around 17 to 1, in contrast to an 85-to-1 ratio in the United States.[8] Interestingly, comparative studies show that in the postwar years Japanese elite voiced more support for low inequality and limiting top incomes than elites of other industrial nations, especially compared to the United States (Verba et al. 1987: 76–85).

Neither are there many families in Japan that are truly wealthy by the standards of other mature capitalist economies; there are few Japanese equivalents to the wealthy Rockefellers, Mellons, Fords, or Morgans. As we saw in the previous chapter, the Mitsui, Nomura, and Fuji families, which would have been equivalents, had most of their wealth taken away after World War II. It is true that a few of the world's most wealthy individuals are Japanese. One 1992 ranking of the world's richest 101 families found 26 to be American and 13 to be Japanese (*Fortune*, June 28, 1993). But even this is misleading because, as noted in the previous chapter, most wealthy people in Japan today are rich because of inflated land prices. However, the very high tax rates on profits from the sale of real estate in Japan, much higher than in the United States, in some ways makes this wealth an illusion.

On the other hand, with respect to status and power inequalities Japan can be said to be one of the most unequal modern industrial societies. The deep bows, very formal and respectful language, and other status rituals given to high-ranking people in Japan, as discussed in Chapter 1, indicate something about the level of status inequalities. As with many other subjects, we find Japan and the

United States almost polar opposites with respect to important aspects of social stratification.

CLASS, STATUS, AND POWER IN JAPAN

It is best to begin an explanation of social stratification in Japan with use of Max Weber's concepts of **class, status,** and **power** (or party). It was of course Weber who offered a **multidimensional view of social stratification** in his criticism of Marx's one-dimensional view (Gerth and Mills 1946: 181–94; Kerbo 1996: 102–4). In addition to Marx's economic dimension of stratification, which emphasized ownership versus nonownership of property as dividing people into different classes, Weber also described the importance of economic divisions based on education and skill level. Then, Weber showed us how divisions based on prestige and honor, or status rankings, and divisions based on power in political organizations and bureaucracies in modern societies are also important, at times more important than economic stratification. Weber stressed that all three dimensions of stratification (class, status, and power or party) will exist in a society, but that one or two of these dimensions will be more important, depending on the kind of stratification system that exists in that society (Kerbo 1996: Chap. 4).

Social stratification in Japan today must be understood with reference to the class and authority dimensions of social stratification as in the United States. However, to a greater extent than in the United States, the status dimension of social stratification is important in Japan. To understand this we must remember that status can be more important in smaller groups and preindustrial societies because these groups have a high level of value consensus.[9] Japan, with a population only about half that of the United States, is not small. However, Japan is made up of people who are 97 to 98 percent racially and ethnically Japanese. They have been strongly socialized into a common value system by the family and schools, and neither religion nor extensive class differences create the kinds of value conflicts in Japan that are found in countries such as the United States (Reischauer and Craig 1978; Verba et al. 1987). Thus, to a far greater extent than Americans, Japanese people tend to agree on who should have higher or lower status, and they readily give deference based on status. Corporate executives in Japan, for example, may have less money than their American counterparts, but they are given enormous respect, which can bring psychological rewards and many other privileges.

Further, as Weber indicated, the status dimension of social stratification is primary in a **caste system,** as in the Indian caste system before British disruption. From about 1615 to 1868 under the Tokugawa shogunate, Japan had something quite like a caste system that in many ways was as rigid as that found in early India. It has been only a little more than 140 years since Japan's Tokugawa caste system fell. Traditions and culture change at a slower pace than social organization or technology. For this reason alone we would expect that status would be a more important dimension of stratification in Japan than in the United States.

WEALTH AND INCOME INEQUALITIES IN POSTWAR JAPAN

As already noted, and as can be seen in Table 5–1, Japanese workers tend to have high incomes compared to the other major industrial

This newly constructed house is the primary residence of the president of one of Japan's top private corporations. It is located in an ordinary neighborhood where one of the authors lived for a time. While luxurious by Tokyo standards, it has no more than 3,000 square feet of interior space, and is a modest home in comparison with the homes of most American top executives.

TABLE 5-1

Comparative Employee and Executive Incomes, 1992

Manufacturing Employees	White-Collar Employees	Managers	CEOs
Germany $36,857	Britain $74,761	Italy $219,573	**United States $717,237**
Canada $34,935	France $62,279	France $190,354	France $479,772
Japan $34,263	Germany $59,916	**Japan $185,437**	Italy $439,441
Italy $31,537	Italy $58,263	Britain $162,190	Britain $439,441
France $30,019	**United States $57,675**	**United States $159,575**	Canada $416,066
United States $27,606	Canada $47,231	Germany $145,627	Germany $390,933
Britain $26,084	**Japan $40,990**	Canada $132,877	**Japan $390,723**

Source: Towers Perrin, *The Wall Street Journal Europe*, October 9, 1992; Mishel and Bernstein (1993), p. 204.

nations, but the top Japanese executives have the lowest incomes. In the United States, it is just the opposite, which of course suggests that inequality is low in Japan and high in the United States. Comparing the average income of the richest 20 percent of people in the society to the average income of the bottom 20 percent of people in the society, Figure 5–1 shows a similar pattern. The income gap in the United States is about 12 to 1 by this measure, whereas the gap for Japan is only 4 to 1. Many other measures of such things as family income show the same pattern: income inequality in Japan is among the lowest of industrial nations, and it is the highest in the United States (Kerbo 1996: Chap. 2).

Considering that material inequalities in Japan were so high before World War II, we should examine how Japan came to be one of the most equal societies with respect to the distribution of income and wealth. Rapid economic growth and low unemployment in recent decades have certainly helped, but this could have also resulted in increased inequality if other factors were not in place. The most

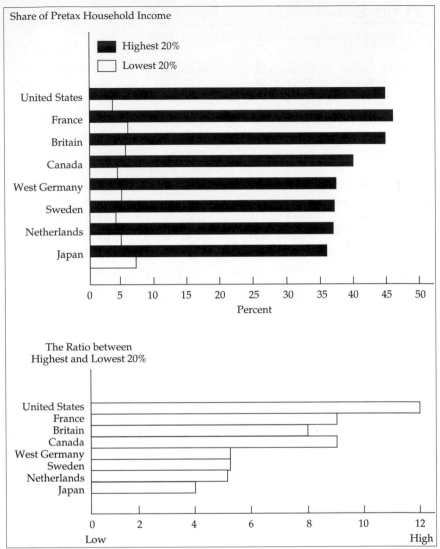

Share of Pretax Household Income

■ Highest 20%
□ Lowest 20%

United States
France
Britain
Canada
West Germany
Sweden
Netherlands
Japan

0 5 10 15 20 25 30 35 40 45 50
Percent

The Ratio between
Highest and Lowest 20%

United States
France
Britain
Canada
West Germany
Sweden
Netherlands
Japan

0   2   4   6   8   10   12
Low   High

FIGURE 5–1 Comparative Income Inequality, leading capitalist nations 1980s
Source: World Bank (1986).

important changes setting the stage for reduced inequality since
World War II are related to reforms or changes made during the few
years the United States remained in control of Japan after World
War II—what are called the Occupation Reforms, in reference to the
U.S. occupation of Japan at the time.

Postwar U.S. Occupation Reforms

At the end of World War II Japan lay in ruins, with a large part of the population living on the brink of starvation. Production was less than 20 percent of what it had been just five years before (Halliday 1975; Johnson 1982; Dore 1987; Lincoln 1988; Reischauer 1988). World War II destroyed lives, property, and social structures in Japan. This set the stage for rebuilding a society that could be different in many ways. Similarly, much the same can be said of Germany. There was, for example, the "equalization of burdens law" in Germany after World War II, which took half the wealth of everyone who had wealth and redistributed it to those who had none (Hoffmeister and Tubach 1992). But it was labor laws giving German workers much influence on the shop floor through "works councils" and half the positions among the corporate boards of directors in every corporation that had the most long-lasting effects on reducing material inequalities (Thelen 1991; Turner 1991). In Japan, changes did not involve labor unions or work laws as much as changes in corporate ownership, land redistribution, and income policies within corporations.

The first of the changes came rather dramatically. As we saw in the previous chapter, on October 8, 1945, two trucks under U.S. Army escort pulled up at the Mitsui corporate headquarters in Tokyo and took away 42 wooden boxes containing $281 million in Mitsui stock belonging to the Mitsui family. After the stock ownership of the other top zaibatsu families was taken, the "Law of the Termination of Zaibatsu" of 1948 took most of the remaining wealth of these and other wealthy families (Roberts 1976: 373–79; Morikawa 1992: 237–40). With little family control of major corporations and much lower wealth inequalities after the war, income inequalities also decreased. Wealth brings income, but so does corporate control, which was lost. Japanese corporate executives today are most often employees and have incomes restricted, as we noted in the previous chapter and will expand on in the next.

A second major economic change involved extensive land reform ordered by the American Occupation. In rural areas these changes had especially beneficial results. Peasants and farmers received land and support from the government, eliminating the long-standing inequality between rural and urban areas. Since then farmers have become relatively well-off in Japan. This has made them a conservative force in politics today, hoping to keep the economic gains they have obtained. (Farmers also hope to prevent redistricting of the political boundaries, which even after the new voting districts created in 1994 gives them about twice as much representation than urban people in the Japanese parliament, the Diet).

In many ways, most important in reducing income inequalities in the postwar period were restraints on high-income demands by those in top positions. The feeling of being part of the homogeneous group (some say the country seems like an extended kinship system) tends to make the Japanese reluctant to ask for big salary increases (Vogel 1971: 160; Abegglen and Stalk 1985: 195; Verba et al. 1987). It is not just corporate executives, however, who have had restraints on wage demands; the devastation brought on by World War II helped create a feeling of unity through common misery, making most people self-conscious of excessive wage demands (Kerbo and McKinstry 1995: Chap. 1). It was in this context that the *nenko* system of setting wages according to age and need was developed, a situation that did not exist before the war (Kalleberg and Lincoln 1988: 126).

Finally, we must recognize that in societies where people are more equal in other ways, and there is little poverty to do damage to children to begin with, there tends to be a more equal income distribution because fewer people fall to the bottom through neglect. With most children well socialized by parents and educated relatively well in standardized public schools, and with few people in minority group status to be discriminated against (as we will see below), especially in the context of a strong economy, more people have a reasonable chance to succeed and achieve decent incomes.

GENDER INEQUALITIES

Relatively low levels of family income and wealth inequality in Japan, however, do not mean equality between the sexes—far from it. Consider some examples: Only 0.1 percent of Japanese corporate executives are women; the percentage of female managers (team leaders, section chiefs, or department heads) was 1.8 percent in 1976, 2.5 percent in 1985, and still only 3.9 percent in 1994 (*Japan Times International Weekly*, August 22, 1994); and of the 15 leading industrial societies, Japan has fewer female college professors than any, with 90 percent male. Even after the 1986 law to reduce discrimination against women, 97 percent of the career-track workers in Japanese companies are men, whereas 99 percent of the temporary clerical employees are women. This is no doubt why there are so many Japanese women who could be called "economic refugees" in the United States. In a big contrast to immigrants from other countries to the United States, 47 percent of the recent Japanese immigrants are well-educated women and most are single.

Sex discrimination has not always been so extensive throughout Japanese history. There have been powerful women and even eight empresses, though the last one ruled in AD 770. (Reischauer and Craig 1978: 16). And in rural areas women have usually experienced less discrimination (Hane 1982: 79).

One of the most important factors that increased the practice of sex discrimination and rigid sex role divisions in Japan was the institutionalization of the samurai (Confucian) values during the Meiji Restoration and the constitution of the late 1800s (Long 1996). Only since World War II and the new constitution have these laws been changed. Since World War II, women in Japan can now vote, own property, start businesses, and even keep their children in the case of divorce (Buckley and Mackie 1986). With this new constitution there has been some slow improvement in opportunities for women in Japan, but traditions are hard to break, and sex discrimination is a fact of life, even though many types of sex discrimination in the workplace are officially prohibited (Cook and Hayashi 1980; Buckley and Mackie 1986; Brinton 1989, 1991). This situation is quite dramatically indicated in Table 5–2, which shows Japan to have the lowest male-to-female income ratio of all industrial societies (a 100 ratio would indicate income equality).

To get another perspective on sex discrimination in Japan, consider an example of what most people would see as a positive aspect of the society, but which, in fact, has a negative side. Japan has the lowest divorce rate of any industrial nation. When we ask why, however, we find that one major reason is the lack of options for women outside of marriage. Career jobs for women in Japan are very limited, the attitudes of men make it difficult for a divorced women to remarry, and welfare benefits are even lower than in the United States. (About 85 percent of the people who get welfare in Japan are elderly or disabled, with only 9 percent single mothers.) However, so as not to suggest that the only way to keep the divorce rate low in a country is to

TABLE 5-2

Comparative Male/Female Income Ratios, 1986–1991

Country	Ratio	Country	Ratio
Iceland	91	Belgium	75
Australia	88	Norway	75
Denmark	83	United States	74
France	82	Germany	73
New Zealand	81	Czechoslovakia	70
Sweden	81	United Kingdom	70
Italy	80	Switzerland	67
Austria	78	Greece	65
Netherlands	77	Luxembourg	63
Finland	76	Canada	63
Portugal	76	Ireland	62
		Japan	50

Source: International Labor Organization, *Yearbook of Labor Statistics,* 1989–90 (Geneva, 1990), pp. 757–65; *United Nations Development Programme,* Human Development Report (New York: Oxford University Press, 1991), p. 179.

limit jobs and careers for women, we should point out that Scandinavian countries have more women in the workplace, with less income disparity to men, and continue to have a low divorce rate, especially compared to the United States. Opportunities for women outside the home, in other words, do not in and of themselves create the higher divorce rates, but the lack of opportunities for women is one factor in Japan.

RACE AND ETHNIC INEQUALITIES

We will give more attention to discrimination against **racial** or **ethnic groups** in Japan in our later chapter on social problems, but here we should consider the issue of inequalities. In one respect, with about 97 to 98 percent of the Japanese population racially and ethnically Japanese, the subject is not quite as important as in the United States (unless of course you are one of these minorities in Japan). But the fact that Japan has serious discrimination against minority groups, when they make up only about 2 to 3 percent of the population, presents an interesting subject. And the interest for sociologists concerns who are the targets of discrimination and the outcomes of this discrimination (such as poverty, low education, and even lower IQ scores) for those involved.

The Case of the Burakumin

One of the most intriguing aspects of discrimination in Japan involves *Burakumin*. More than any other case, this shows that racial and biological explanations of inequality of all kinds have no merit. As recently as 1980, some 70 percent of the Japanese people maintained that Burakumin are a different race (Hane 1982: 139). Burakumin, however, are racially and even ethnically Japanese in every way; but they have been treated with extreme discrimination, leading to many kinds of social problems for these people.

Although their history is not completely clear, it seems that Burakumin were former outcaste members of the quasi-caste system that existed in Tokugawa Japan (1600s to 1863) and ever before. With the fall of the Tokugawa shogunate, the modernization efforts of the new Meiji government led to elimination of their legal status as outcastes in 1871.

Today it is estimated there are about 2 million Japanese with Burakumin background. They continue to experience discrimination, even though one must look very hard to find out that a person has this family background. But many in Japan do look hard. Before marrying someone or hiring a new employee, for example, it is common to have a detective agency check the background of the person for Burakumin ancestors. The continued preoccupation with Burakumin by Japan is not surprising to social theorists, however. As Coser (1956, 1967), among others, has pointed out, when there is a strong sense of in-group and an emphasis on conformity in any society, there seems to be a need for an out-group on which to look down. The Burakumin have long filled this role in Japanese society.

Most interesting for sociologists is that studies of these minority groups, especially Burakumin, show that the material and psychological effects of discrimination are similar to those found among minorities in the United States (De Vos and Wagatsuma 1966; Lee and De Vos 1981). Discrimination leads to poverty and psychological problems of self-identity and self-evaluation, which further lead to lower education, delinquency, and more poverty. In other words, there is a cycle of discrimination leading to lower achievement. Again, this situation is most interesting with Burakumin. These people are not racially or biologically different from other Japanese, but their IQ scores are much lower, fewer go on to college compared to other Japanese, they are three times more likely to be arrested, and 5 percent of them are on welfare compared to only 2 percent of other Japanese (*New York Times*, November 30, 1995). Even though race and ethnic differences are not factors with Burakumin, we find a situation very similar to racial minorities in the United States (such as lower average IQ scores), which strongly suggests the problem all over the world is racism and discrimination, not biological differences, in contrast to what has been suggested in the controversial book *The Bell Curve* by Herrnstein and Murray (1994).

We must note, though, that efforts by the Japanese government and other organizations such as the Burakumin Liberation League have had much success recently in reducing such discrimination. For example, the Japanese government is making it more difficult to identify the Burakumin background of people by requiring all old family records of this status to be eliminated or restricted to access by relatives only. In some areas of cities, such as one in Kobe where in 1980 all residents were Burakumin, there are now as many as 50 percent non-Burakumin living there. And as many as 70 percent of Burakumin marriages are to non-Burakumin today (*New York Times*, November 30, 1995). Also, Japanese government affirmative action programs are paying off in education. For example, $29 billion in scholarships since 1969 have gone specifically to Burakumin. About 20 years ago, Burakumin children had a rate of college attendance 35 percent below the average; now it is only 11 percent below average (*Los Angeles Times*, January 2, 1993).

Two other groups that are the targets of extensive discrimination in Japan are Koreans (considered in more detail in Chapter 11) and a smaller population of Chinese who live there. Both groups came to Japan primarily in the twentieth century, with most Chinese coming from Taiwan, a Japanese colony from 1895 until the end of World War II. Koreans also came to Japan primarily after Japan took control of Korea in 1910, with many coming as forced laborers in mines during World War II. Again, although discrimination is decreasing, studies of Koreans reveal outcomes of discrimination such as low income, lower education, and many other social problems.

SOCIAL MOBILITY IN JAPAN

In every society one of the most important questions about social stratification is related to equality of opportunity—What are people's chances of moving up or down the stratification system, and why? This is the subject of **social mobility.** We can be brief here because in many ways research on this subject has shown that there are few differences between the United States and Japan, and among advanced industrial societies in general for that matter (Ishida 1993). In most advanced industrial societies there has been a fair amount of social mobility up stratification levels from one generation to the next, at least for those not too low in the stratification system. In other words, individuals tend to be higher in the class system than were their parents (Kerbo 1996: Chap. 11).

There are, however, some interesting differences in social mobility in Japan when compared to the United States. For example, there is somewhat more social mobility upward from lower-class positions in Japan (Naoi and Ojima 1989; Ishida, Goldthorpe, and Erikson 1987). The rate of working-class inheritance of a father's class position (staying in the same class as one's father) is 21 percent in Japan, which is especially low compared to the 39 to 78 percent for Europe (depending on which country).

It appears that much of the mobility out of the working class and into middle-class positions in Japan is related to Japan's recent and rapid growth. Japan's industrialization started after that of Europe and the United States, allowing it to copy some advanced technology during its industrial takeoff. Japan therefore skipped over some of the early stages of industrialization that create more working-class jobs.

As we will see in our later chapter on education, since World War II there have been more equal opportunities for educational achievement in Japan. Good public schools are more accessible to all children in Japan than in the United States, and relatively fair examinations strictly determine who is able to get into the best high schools and universities (Rohlen 1983), leading to higher occupational attainment. Thus, the intelligent and hardworking son or daughter of a working-class family can expect more equal chances to get into the better universities in Japan than in the United States, though as we will see in our chapter on education, the advantages of being in a family with enough money to allow attendance at "cram schools" after regular school hours is starting to erode the previously high equality of educational opportunity in Japan.

Finally, one of the most important reasons there has been somewhat more social mobility in Japan since World War II, however, has been the simple fact that there is less overall inequality in Japan than in the United States. The gap between the better-off and the low-income families is less, with fewer people at the very bottom of the stratification system who have no money for schooling, who must work full-time at an early age just to help keep food on the table, and who have other disadvantages of low-income people in America, such as poorer health and lower academic ability due to poor diet and neglect by parents worried about keeping food on the table (Kerbo 1996: Chap. 9).

CONCLUSION

In this chapter we have considered how social stratification in Japan is similar and also different in many ways from that in the United States. In particular, we have seen how the status dimension of stratification is more important in Japan, resulting in more status inequality; but material inequalities, such as income, are much lower in Japan than in the United States. We then examined the level of gender inequality in Japan, which is extensive, and the nature of racial and ethnic inequalities, especially the interesting case of the Burakumin. Finally, we reviewed the subject of social mobility and found few differences between Japan and the United States.

When asked which class they belong to, more people in Japan than in the United States say they are middle class; in fact, about 90 percent claim this status. Social stratification and class position in Japan, however, have certainly not disappeared. In a country in which people don't like to admit being much different from their fellow citizens, claiming to be middle class is one of the most politically correct responses (Ishida 1993). There are still people in Japan who must labor in working-class jobs with less pay than middle-class employees throughout the large government and corporate bureaucracies of Japan and top managers and higher-skill professional people.

In contrast to the United States, however, there are two important differences with respect to social stratification in Japan. First, material things such as income and wealth are less unequally distributed. Second, status inequalities are greater in Japan. Seldom is a person able to treat another as equal because of the importance of rankings based on such things as age, education, and occupation. In this chapter we have provided some of the reasons for these differences and their consequences for people living in the first advanced industrial society in Asia.

CHAPTER 6

The Japanese Power Elite

One of our key points in the chapter on social stratification was the contrasting low material inequality but high status inequality in Japan; the United States is the opposite on both accounts. But there is another interesting contrast: Japan has a powerful and interlocked group of men at the top of the corporate economy and government ministry that guides the nation's political economy to a greater degree than found in the United States or Europe today.

As C. Wright Mills in the famous book *The Power Elite* (1956) noted many years ago, one cannot fully understand what happens in a country, where that country is going, or the position of the men and women in that country without understanding the nature of its power elite. In this regard, Mills argued that a set of three groups of elite—the corporate rich, top government officials, and top military officials—dominated the political and economic system of the United States in the 1950s. Ironically, though Mills was writing about the United States, in many ways his description of a power elite fits Japan even better (Kerbo and McKinstry 1995), with certainly the exception of the military.

What is often referred to as *the iron triangle* in Japan is made up of the top managers of the biggest corporations in Japan, the men on top of the government bureaucratic ministries, and leading politicians. Most agree, however, that the first two groups are most important, especially in the last few years of political turmoil and scandal among Japanese politicians. In this chapter we will examine each of these elite groups in Japan and the extent of their unity, which many people think makes them far more powerful than elites in other industrial societies. Then we will consider some of the implications of these elites for the future of Japan.

THE CORPORATE ELITE

The base for the corporate elite in Japan is the corporate groupings of the biggest corporations, the keiretsu. Virtually all of the biggest corporations in Japan are linked to one of a few big keiretsu. Usually singled out are the big six keiretsu groups: the Mitsubishi Group, Mitsui Group, Sumitomo Group, Fuji Group, Daiichi Kangyo Group, and Sanwa Group (Ōsono 1991; Gerlach 1992; Kerbo and McKinstry 1995; Chap. 4).

The Mitsui Group provides a good example of how keiretsu operate: there are 24 companies that form the center of this keiretsu, including many Mitsui companies, along with Toshiba, Toyota, Mitsukoshi department stores (among the biggest in Japan), and Japan Steel. As with the other keiretsu, a major means of linkage is common stock ownership. This is to say that, for example, Mitsui Bank holds considerable stock in Toyota (often about 20 to 25 percent of the company's stock), as well as Toshiba, Mitukoshi, Japan Steel, and the others. At the same time, Toyota and the others hold considerable stock in Mitsui Bank as well as in each other. In this manner, these companies have a big stake in each other and will of course work together to protect common interests.

There are still other important links among the keiretsu. As noted previously, each of the major keiretsu has what are translated as "presidents' clubs," which meet regularly to discuss common issues in the economy and politics. Above separate keiretsu links, however, there is an even more powerful means of coordinating political activities among all of the biggest corporations in Japan. *Keidanren*, or the "Japan Federation of Economic Organizations," is a kind of superbusiness establishment, or as some say, the "parliament of big business," with the Keidanren chairman referred to as the "prime minister" of business—and most likely the most powerful man in Japan (Kakuma 1981; Okumura 1983; Atsuta 1992). (Beginning in

1994 that person has been Shoichiro Toyoda, former president and chairman of Toyota Motors.) The approximately 900 members of Keidanren are from the biggest corporations, across all of the big keiretsu groups. These people meet often to discuss common problems, form political lobbying activities to pressure the Japanese government to protect their interests, and decide which politicians are to be given campaign funds. (As noted earlier, about 90 percent of these campaign funds have gone to the Liberal Democratic Party politicians, and when these funds were withdrawn in 1993, the LDP lost control of the Diet.)

THE MINISTRY ELITE

Unlike in the United States, and to a greater degree than in European nations, the power of the Japanese government resides more with the career civil servants at the top of the most important government ministries, rather than with the politicians. The minister of each of these main ministries, such as the Ministry of International Trade and Industry (MITI), Ministry of Finance, Ministry of Foreign Affairs, and so forth, are not the most powerful people; rather, it is the administrative vice minister of each agency who is most powerful. The minister is a political appointee, much like cabinet secretaries in the United States, usually a politician, and stays with the agency only a brief time. The administrative vice minister, on the other hand, is a career minister, is very well educated and experienced, and has been with the agency for his (seldom her) whole career since graduating from a university. The administrative vice ministers in Japan, in other words, are rather independent from elected politicians and are experts in their respective fields (Johnson 1982, 1995; Koh 1989; van Wolferen 1989; Kerbo and McKinstry 1995: Chap. 5).

JAPANESE POLITICIANS

The politicians in top positions in the Diet (parliament) are not now, nor were they ever, powerless. Among other things, laws must be passed—even if mostly written by ministry officials—and tax revenues must be allocated. But the postwar Japanese political elite can be best described as playing a supportive role for the corporate and ministry elite, and as we have already said, the political elite are only a weak third member of the iron triangle of elites in Japan today.

From the late 1980s, however, the political elite have become even weaker because of several major corruption scandals and a growing mistrust by the public. Before 1993, and going back to 1955, the political elite from one political party—the Liberal Democratic Party—dominated Japanese politics, winning every national election in that almost 40-year period. But finally they became so corrupt and an embarrassment to their corporate elite supporters that the party lost control of the Diet in 1993.

Campaign reform laws passed in 1993 and 1994 have created many changes in the election process. But during the next national election of October 1996, little changed. The LDP continues to be most powerful, though still with a coalition government; and although the major campaign issues in 1996 were too much government regulation and the power of the ministry elite, almost nothing has been done to change these situations since the 1996 elections.

ELITE UNITY

Since World War II, cooperation, coordination, and unity have become even more common among the iron triangle of Japanese elite (Kerbo and McKinstry 1995: Chap. 7). There are several powerful means of unity that bring the Japanese elite together far more than elites of the United States or Europe today. Among these means are the exchange of personnel across the three elite groups, old school ties, intermarriage, and to a much lesser extent, social clubs.

The extensive practice of *amakudari* is among the most important means of elite interlock and unity. Translated as something like "to descend from heaven," amakudari refers to the common early retirement of powerful ministry officials who then move "down" to top corporate positions (Usui and Colignon 1994). During 1991 alone, 215 individuals who were members of the bureaucratic elite left their government positions for new corporate positions in companies regulated by the very ministry from which these individuals "retired." Of these 215 individuals, 54 came from the Ministry of Finance (see *Japan Quarterly*, July–September 1992: 414). Table 6–1 provides a list of the number of amakudari employees in top positions in the 100 largest corporations in Japan and the ministry from which they came.

TABLE 6-1

Amakudari Officials in the Top 100 Corporations

From Ministry of Finance	151
From MITI	118
From Ministry of Development	74
From Ministry of Transportation	65
From Bureau of the Environment	40
From Postal Service	34
From Bureau of Defence	33
Other	55

Source: Kerbo and McKinstry (1995), Chap. 7; Okumura (1978).

Another key means of elite unity, *old school ties*, is centered on the nature of the Japanese educational system. A small number of universities in Japan are considered most prestigious and are most important to enter for gaining elite status later, with Tokyo University, Todai for short, by far the most important. For Japan, Tokyo University is somewhat like Harvard, Yale, Princeton, Cambridge, and Oxford all in one. It is very difficult to pass the examination to get into Tokyo University, which also means that the elite members thus selected are certainly among the brightest in Japan and therefore given more legitimacy once they are in elite positions. But it also means that friendship ties formed while at Tokyo University will be carried throughout their lives, creating extensive elite unity. Some of the graduates will go to Sony, some to Toyota, some to Sumitomo Bank, and still others to places such as the Ministry of Finance, MITI, and the Foreign Ministry. But wherever they go, these old school ties will keep them unified and working together (Kerbo and McKinstry 1995: Chap. 8).

With respect to the bureaucratic elite, a 1991 study showed that 59 percent of all recent graduates entering the fast track to top ministry positions were Todai graduates (*Japan Times International Weekly*, March 9–15, 1992: 6). A 1981 study found that with one exception, all of the heads of the most powerful ministry (administrative vice ministers) were Todai graduates (Kitagawa and Kainuma 1985). In the most influential government ministry of all, the Finance Ministry, during the late 1970s, 89 percent of all top officials above the section chief level were Todai graduates.

Among the corporate elite we find the same pattern. One survey of the 154 top industrial elite found 45 percent were Todai graduates (Miyake et al. 1985). In the powerful big business organization, Keidanren, six of the eight chairmen since 1946 have been Todai graduates (Atsuta 1992). Moreover, in the top three offices in each of the top 10 banks in Japan, 19 of the 30 executives were Todai graduates, with the same pattern found in all types of industries in Japan (see data compiled by Kerbo and McKinstry 1995: Chap. 8, from Kakuma 1981).

For the political elite, we find much the same pattern, especially for top LDP members and prime ministers. Of the 18 prime ministers from the Liberal Democratic Party from 1946 to 1993, 10 have been graduates from Tokyo University, most from its Law School (Hayakawa 1983; Kitagawa and Kainuma 1985; Jin 1989).

It is not simply having attended Todai, and especially its law school, that is important. Because of the Japanese system of age ranking, people of the same age reach the very top of all types of elite positions at about the same time in Japan. This means these people in top positions in corporations, the ministry, and politics at any one point in time were most likely classmates or even roommates when they were college students. But there are still other means of unity.

Much like Domhoff (1979, 1983) has shown for the United States, *social and business clubs* in Japan also function to tie the elite together (Harada 1988; Sato 1990; Kerbo and McKinstry 1995: Chap. 7). One of the most exclusive is the Tokyo Lawn Tennis Club, though the Tokyo Riding Club, the Tokyo Golf Club, and the Kōjunsha must also be included. Such social and business clubs are perhaps somewhat less important in Japan, however, because Japanese executives often have less spare time than their American counterparts. Still, clubs in Japan, especially the golf clubs, serve an important function for unity among the elite and are places where elite can mingle to make political and economic deals as well as discuss common problems.

Finally, one rather unique means of unity can be described with the following example: Six of the postwar prime ministers, about a dozen corporate elite, several ministry elite, and even the late Emperor Hirohito's brother and sister have something in common besides being among the inner circle of elite—they were all directly related through marriage (Hayakawa 1983; Jin 1989). There is a common practice of *intermarriage* among the Japanese elite, which creates powerful family alliances called *keibatsu*. Some Japanese social scientists presenting data on such family alliances claim that about 40 keibatsu, or extended families, dominate the Japanese corporate economy and government (Kerbo and McKinstry 1995: Chap. 7).

The means of creating these keibatsu family links are also interesting. There are private groups and individuals, along with relatives, who specialize in matchmaking among elite families (Hamabata 1990). And much more than in the rest of the Japanese population, the elite families use the old tradition of arranged marriages to form such family alliances or marry their offspring to influential people. For example, one practice today is for such matchmakers to identify and introduce to elite families the up-and-coming young men in the powerful ministry. There are even publications identifying such young men for interested elite families. An arranged marriage with one of these men can have very useful benefits when the man moves to the top of the ministry in later years or retires early to join the company of his in-laws to use the ministry ties of his earlier years. And on top of all this, a common practice is for such a young man to be formally adopted by the parents of his wife, thus becoming what is called *yoshi*, and taking over as head of the family line in his later years.

CONCLUSION

In this chapter we have examined the nature of Japan's power elite, the famous iron triangle. We examined the base of power for the corporate elite, the ministry elite, and the political elite. We then examined various ways the elite are united, such as through the exchange of personnel (amakudari), old school ties, and formation of keibatsu via marriage.

Taken together, the above information indicates that C. Wright Mills's (1956) idea of a power elite does seem to apply more in Japan than in the United States. We should emphasize that the study of elite, their power, unity, and backgrounds, is not just an academic exercise, as Mills's was among the first to point out. Elite with independent power, unchecked by democratic forces from below, can lead a nation into war or peace, economic disaster or reform, when it is in their best interests, irrespective of the interests of others in the nation. Before

World War II, for example, it was one set of powerful elite that pushed Japan into war with China, and then the United States, for what they thought would be the greater glory of Japan, while the rest of the population knew little of their plans.

Today, after extensive political corruption in recent years and an economy that no longer seems able to maintain its competitive edge in the world, there is increasing discontent among the Japanese people. There are as well some indications that the low postwar income and wealth in Japan is changing, producing more inequality, which has further created discontent among the Japanese people. But despite needed changes, very few have been forthcoming in Japan. At present the set of elite we have described are unwilling to make the changes that will upset their power. Corporate elite have started pushing the ministry and political elite for some change favoring their corporate interests, but it is too early to tell if the split will widen, reducing the iron triangle's power over Japan, thus bringing about change.

CHAPTER 7

The Family

Kinship and family ties have played a fundamental role in human society for as long as human society has existed. Kinship systems have been a basic form of identity throughout history; family ties are part of important social regulations, such as providing a way of passing on possessions to another generation. In the modern world family life is an area of intimacy, a private place away from the larger society. Perhaps the most important role of family is the raising of children. Other institutions for raising children have occasionally been tried, but family life in some form has been a convenient and logical choice for the way societies have managed the early socialization of children throughout time and in every place.

Species other than humans commonly have a form of family life as well, but only human beings, among all the creatures we know about, live by cultural traits and not primarily by following instinctive patterns. The great advantage of culture as a foundation of behavior is that it is flexible, and family life for people everywhere, while meeting similar needs and providing basic required functions, is to a great extent customized to meet the demands of particular situations. Because the possibilities of social organization are limited, similar situations often result in similar types of family and kinship models. A description of family life in Japan demonstrates how the overall patterns of family tend to adapt to other changes in society;

that is, individual societies develop their own versions of these broad patterns.

THE JAPANESE FAMILY

The major cities of all modern societies look very much alike, and compared with their grandparents, the people who live in them live similar lives in many respects; people who live in industrial societies all over the world share a great deal, regardless of differences in things such as language and religion. A typical Japanese family and a typical American family have many things in common. For the members of each to live for a time in a household of the other would not be all that difficult; in fact, university students from both countries experience just such exchanges all the time. It is also true that over time family themes in Japan have become more like those of the West as they share more of the aspects of modern life together.

However, no society today, regardless of level of economic development, is either all modern or all traditional. Even the most advanced industrial societies mix the baggage of cultural history together with pressures to adjust to the present, and in this way blend tradition and modernity. Looking at the kinship and family system of Japan, we see immediately a considerable amount of conformity to some basic needs of life in the post-industrial world, but we also notice more traditional aspects than in contemporary Europe or the United States. Japan did not experience industrialization until a little over 100 years ago, a full century and a half after parts of Europe had begun to go through those particular kinds of changes. And unlike the United States, Japan is not a transplanted culture; its cultural roots go deeply into the soil right where the Japanese live today.

If we look at the broad sweep of history over the past several thousand years it is easy to witness the close connection between family systems and the basic economic organization of societies (Lenski, Lenski, and Nolan 1991). When some societies of the world developed horticulture, or gardening, as their basic support system, they formed clan structures because of the need for more formalized decision making. As large sections of human population embraced modern plow agriculture, once again the kind of family system that best met economic needs evolved, and the **extended family** was born. As plow agriculture slowly replaced other forms of subsistence agriculture starting around 6,000 years ago, the extended family came to be the most common family system throughout the world. With industrialization and capitalism, however, things like a money economy, social and geographic mobility, urban life in general, and the growth of government influence over everyday life tend to diminish the vitality of the extended family system. Two or three hundred years before the Industrial Revolution, which was the death knell for the extended family in the West, **patrilineal** kinship groups had already began to slowly be replaced by the smaller nuclear or conjugal family system. In such a system, which modern societies gravitate to, there is more emphasis on a married couple and their dependent children, with less emphasis on the connection to vertical blood ties though the male line.

An aspect of Japan in the modern world that makes it a little different from other modern nations is that the extended family system, only a dim historical memory for most Europeans and Americans, is something many Japanese 60 or 70 years old grew up with. The movement toward a nuclear family system, with all the changes it eventually brings to a society, only started for most Japanese one or two generations ago (Morgan and Hirosima 1983). Because remnants of the extended family system exert more influence over modern life in Japan than in other industrialized societies, we should review the nature of that system in detail.

THE EXTENDED FAMILY IN JAPANESE HISTORY

For more than 1,000 years, until well into the twentieth century, central to Japanese family and kinship ties was the Japanese version of the patrilineal extended family. From the area a little south of modern Tokyo on to the north, this family system was called *ie*, pronounced something like the American slang word, "yeah." In southern and western Japan, most frequently this family system was called *dōzoku*. The ie is a patrilineal extended family system in which the oldest son, and perhaps the next one or two sons in succession, stay as adults at home and run the farm or other enterprise, while other sons born after them move off to form branches of the main family. Women leave their own family of birth and become official members of their husband's ie. We call this kind of patrilineal family unit "extended" because it is a larger family grouping than the nuclear family that became the norm in northern and western Europe a couple of hundred years ago. It includes the oldest living members of a single family, at least one grown son, his wife, all young children, and the oldest male children even after marriage. Extended families, except for a small ruling elite and perhaps a few other privileged aristocrats, are units of production. Most people in societies with that type of family arrangement are peasant farmers, and although they may not all live in the same household, the extended family is the basic social unit for organizing work, teaching children, carrying out religious rituals, and most of the rhythms of everyday life.

The description of the Japanese ie is similar to that of extended families all over the world, from contemporary Iran to rural Mexico to the Italy of two or three generations ago. An overriding characteristic of the extended family system is an exaggerated gap in **gender** roles. Men and women are treated almost like separate species, with women relegated to almost complete concentration on the domestic details of raising children and running the household. Men are officially supreme in this kind of family arrangement; only men inherit permanent family membership at birth. Women join a family from the outside through marriage and are only accepted as real members by having children, especially male children. As they grow older, the women come to actually run the extended family household, although they must defer to the men of the family in matters outside the home. New brides play a role similar to recruits in the military; they take orders, do most of the work around the house, and are at the beck and call of their husband's mother.

In most versions of the extended family, emotional ties between husband and wife are not usually very strong, being far outweighed by ties between a husband and his own parents. As people get older, their power and prestige in the family tend to increase, and when they retire from active work they stay in the household playing a role akin to elderly counselors. Marriages bind one extended family to another and so are a matter for the family heads to consider carefully, with the young principals having in most cases little to say in the matter.

Human beings are not robots, and even though all extended family systems contain certain basic similarities, they of course show differences from society to society. In some interesting ways, Japan by coincidence was more similar to Europe than to the rest of Asia in matters of kinship. For example, as virtually all European societies have traditionally been monogamous, Japan has also been characterized by monogamy. Wealthy and powerful Japanese men have had concubines, and in modern times mistresses, but never multiple wives with full legal status of married spouses as was the case in traditional China and many parts of southern Asia.

Japan was not as influenced by Confucianism as were China and Korea, and the intense consciousness of family lines in traditional China—"ancestor worship," as people outside China often call it—did not take root in Japan, except at the very top of the social order. Until a little over 100 years ago most Japanese didn't even use a family name. One reason modernization occurred with such ease in Japan, compared with the rest of Asia, was that the traditional family system there did not get in the way as much. Bureaucratic administration practices, necessary for new ways of organizing the economy and government, did not have to fight against strong family ties as hard in Japan as in other Asian societies. Japanese people, for example, have always regarded cousins with about the same degree of importance as have the British or other Western Europeans—recognized as part of a family entity, but not people one must accommodate in almost every situation ahead of nonrelatives as was the case in traditional China and in other societies of Asia.

THE CHANGING JAPANESE FAMILY

The culture of any society has to be taught to each new generation anew. The immense volume to human culture complicates the task of passing it on, even more so in the modern world because cultural items keep changing during the lifetime of a single person. Ideas of how family life is supposed to be structured and how families are supposed to work are of course a fundamental part of any cultural system. When changing circumstances bring pressure for change in the images of family life, many other things begin to change; when they change very rapidly, there is bound to be some amount of ambiguity and confusion. Although most Japanese households are as harmonious and mutually supportive of individuals as in other societies, if we look carefully we can see evidence of friction as one family system replaces another, right before our eyes so to speak.

Today in Japan, the word *ie* is hardly ever used to mean family. Nowadays Japanese use the word *kazoku*, which for most people has come to have a meaning very similar to the English word *family*.

Kazoku for the most part is seen as a residence unit: children, parents, and perhaps grandparents. The breadwinner, the person in the unit who provides the most income (it is almost always a man in his middle years), together with his or her spouse, tend to be the main decision makers. Even farm families, considered to be more resistant to change than city dwellers, and with a very high percentage of live-in grandparents, have for the most part also adopted the modern kazoku. Older members of farm families no longer have the power over the rest of the family that they once enjoyed, young people are about as free to pick their own marriage partners as are Japanese living in cities, and few brides of farmers would put up with being considered servants of their mothers-in-law the way they used to be.

We should remember, however, that the shift from ie to kazoku has in historical terms been rather sudden and rather recent. Cultural change is rarely well coordinated, especially since some are liberated by the change, others disadvantaged. One way of looking at it would be to observe that when things begin to significantly change, some people get the message, some don't. Within the Japanese family system, some people, especially old people, still harbor within the definition of kazoku elements left over from ie. Old people resented for meddling in the lives of their grown children can be a much more severe problem in Japan precisely because the issue is not completely resolved. When aged men and women live with their children in the United States and Europe, unless they are personally wealthy, it is usually quite clear that it is they, the old people, who live in their children's home, and it is the children's decision to share their resources with their parents. Under the rules of the old ie, of course, no matter who provided the actual income, the oldest male was the official head of the family, old people were the major decision makers, and taking care of the older generation was an immutable obligation that adult children had to bear.

Remnants of the ie are easiest to maintain in three generational residence units. Although three generations living together under one roof is still the ideal in Japan, fewer and fewer Japanese families are able to actually do so (Morgan and Hirosima 1983). As we have already seen, with a population about half that of the United States, the total landmass of Japan is less than that of California, and more than 80 percent of the total area is so mountainous that use for agriculture or dwellings is very limited. The bulk of the Japanese population today is crowded together in towns and cities in the few coastal plains available. That kind of crowding together of people makes space an extremely important commodity. Although some houses in rural and suburban Japan are quite roomy, the average Japanese family lives in houses and apartments very small by the standards of the rest of the developed world. There simply is not enough space for the older generation to live with adult children in small urban residences of 600 or 700 square feet, about the size of a single-bedroom apartment in the United States.

In fact, taking care of the oldest generation looms as a huge problem in Japan's future, a problem the government is trying its best to deal with, as we shall see in more detail in Chapter 12. Japanese live longer than people in any other large society. The nation also has a quite low birthrate, averaging less than 1.5 children per family. Early in the twenty-first century, one of every five Japanese will be over the age of 65. At present, the percentage of elderly Japanese provided for in nursing homes is small, but that number will greatly expand.

GENDER ROLES AND COURTSHIP

Another way in which the shift to the modern kazoku has brought about adjustments in Japan, along with some confusion and friction, can be seen in relations between husbands and wives. The role of wife and mother in Japan has a more traditional feel than in most other developed societies. The ideal of women forgoing any kind of career in favor of a life of devotion to husband and family is still strongly supported in the Japanese popular imagination. The legal system is slowly beginning to support some amount of flexibility in the ideal of feminine domesticity, but even today, a women is removed from the family register she was born into and transferred to the register of her husband's family on marriage, reflecting the old ie premise that a wife "belonged" to her husband's lineage. For this reason, until as late as 1982, a foreign woman married to a Japanese man could rather easily obtain Japanese citizenship, whereas it was next to impossible for a foreign husband of a Japanese woman to become a Japanese citizen.

Courtship, which sociology defines as the ways people come together for purposes of marriage, also is still in many ways influenced by ideas rooted in ie. Many young Japanese have a rather strong sense of denial concerning the effect of tradition over matters of courtship; they prefer to think that they are as modern as their counterparts in Europe or North America. But even though many Japanese do indeed follow courtship practices that deviate little from those of other industrialized societies, one does not have to look very hard to see the unmistakable weight of the past in what goes on between young unmarried people. For example, although the amount of dating and premarital sex in Japan probably does not differ very much from common practices elsewhere, when it comes to the actual act of marriage, a certain seriousness sets in that is not as common in Europe or the United States. By seriousness we mean simply that the implications of what is happening in a prospective marriage are more soberly considered, and not just by the two young people themselves. The emotions of romance as a factor of courtship play a far greater role than in the past, but they have never in Japan come to be as paramount in pairing off for marriage as in, say, the United States.

Even today, almost a third of marriages are the result of what the Japanese call *omiai*, a formal meeting between people of marriageable age arranged by someone else (Long 1996). Somebody, perhaps a relative of one of them, an older friend or work mate, sometimes even a professor who knew both of them as students, schedules a meeting between the two people. Formerly an omiai took place in the go-between's residence, but far more common today is one that takes place in a private room in a rather exclusive restaurant. Parents either are in attendance, or if not, and the meeting goes well (meaning the two people agree to begin seeing each other in earnest consideration of marriage), both sets of parents are introduced rather early on.

Japanese distinguish a marriage that begins with an omiai from virtually the only other pattern available, a *renai kekkon*, literally "love marriage." But that label should not mislead anyone into thinking that people who find each other on their own enjoy the autonomy of those typical in Western societies. Families, and in particular, parents, still usually have far more veto power in Japan over a prospective marriage than all but parents of the very rich in the West. When their children seem to be having romantic connections to someone whose family background they are unfamiliar with, parents still often turn to the services of people involved in a thriving industry in Japan: private investigators who specialize in checking out family circumstances.

Japanese parents have more power over whom their children marry for several reasons beyond the lingering ideas of marriage as a link between families held over from ie. Although the average age at marriage in Japan is about two years older than in the United States, Americans marry at a wide range of ages. In contrast, almost everyone in Japan marries while still young, before the onset of financial independence. Weddings in Japan are very standardized; almost everyone has the same kind of ceremony, which have come to be huge productions requiring staggering amounts of money. Weddings now average a total expense of around $60,000. Without the help of family, of course, it would be impossible to carry off such an expensive affair. Also, far more than in the United States, young women, and even a surprisingly high percentage of young men, have never had a personal address outside their parents' home until after marriage. Many young Americans and Europeans in their 20s are already living far from home for most of the year, thus making the ties that bind them and their parents a little weaker than Japanese even several years their senior.

THE JAPANESE NUCLEAR FAMILY TODAY

Family life would appear to be more stable in Japan than in the United States; divorce, for example is only about one-fifth as likely between Japanese couples as for Americans, as indicated in Table 7–1. It should not be assumed that there is necessarily less conflict within Japanese family circles, however. As in previous times in the West, a Japanese wife is supposed to bear with circumstances that would routinely cause divorce in the United States, including perhaps the husband's repeated sexual affairs with other women, his perpetual drunkenness, or even physical beating. Not all Japanese wives do bear with these things, of course, but divorce is less an option for most because of the difficulty divorced women have in supporting themselves and their children in Japan.

Companionship between spouses is not nearly as emphasized in Japan as in many Western societies. Even in a harmonious Japanese family, husbands and wives tend to have separate friends and, to a great extent, separate social lives; thus living together without being very intimate seems to be a bit easier for both spouses to tolerate. As indicated in Table 7–2, Japanese couples are much less likely to say

TABLE 7-1

Comparative Divorce Rates per 1,000 Population, 1988–1989

Country	Divorce Rate	Country	Divorce Rate
United States	4.8%	Norway	2.1%
Soviet Union	3.4	Germany	2.1
Canada	3.1	Austria	2.0
Denmark	3.0	Switzerland	1.9
United Kingdom	2.9	Netherlands	1.9
Finland	2.9	Belgium	1.9
New Zealand	2.6	France	1.9
Australia	2.4	Japan	1.3
Sweden	2.3	Italy	0.4

Source: United Nations, *Demographic Yearbook,* 1989; Shapiro (1992), p. 36.

TABLE 7-2

Percentage of Couples Saying Sex Is Important in a Marriage

Country	% Saying Very Important
United States	75.6%
Canada	75.2
United Kingdom	73.8
France	71.9
Italy	71.8
Netherlands	69.3
Germany	55.5
Japan	35.3

Source: World Values Survey, Shapiro (1992), p. 47.

sex is a key to a successful marriage. It is not that there is any more tension necessarily between married people. The average Japanese couple is quite comfortable spending time together, and the present generation of newlyweds seems to be putting more emphasis on life between spouses. But it is true that most Japanese, including probably even most young people, consider that Americans and Europeans spend an excessive amount of time doing things together as married partners. This is especially true for Japanese men, who would no doubt find it painful to give up the many evening and weekend hours spent cavorting with male friends if they were to try to live the life of a typical middle-class American man.

Needless to say, most Americans would not approve of the ideals surrounding married life in Japan. Just as in courtship practices, the roles of husband and wife in the minds of most Japanese are influenced by the past, and the traditional ideal for wives in Japan still exerts considerable influence over actual behavior. According to that ideal, a woman should dedicate her life to husband and children. If she works outside the home, it should be solely to boost family income, and at the birth of her first child, typically within a year or so of marriage, she should give up most outside involvement to become a superdomestic homemaker. The ideal holds that a woman should not in any way threaten the primacy of her husband's role as head of family; she should be demure, gentle, and patient, the support pillar for other family members. All this makes Japanese women sound like servants, but the traditional ideal is under considerable pressure for change. Women have made important advancements in many professions, and while still well behind their counterparts in the United States, they are beginning to be represented more and more in the world outside the home.

Even for those women who follow the more familiar practice of homemaker, however, there is a considerable degree of misunderstanding concerning the role of Japanese wife and mother outside of Japan. It is absolutely true that Japanese women are something like second-class citizens in the world of work. They are less likely to achieve important positions in the corporate world than in any other industrial nation. At work in large organizations, women wear uniforms and have an image only a little above that of office servants. Even at home, symbols of male privilege are still much in evidence. Most men in Japan, even the youngest generation of workers, perform almost no domestic chores whatsoever, expecting to be virtually waited on by their wives. However, the position women play within the family is in some ways more powerful than that played by their counterparts in the West. Men are the official heads of most families in Japan, but women there are in charge of family matters more firmly than in the United States or Europe.

A tradition developed in the modern Japanese family that placed financial matters—planning, most purchases, saving—almost exclusively with wives. Older children jokingly refer to their mother as *ōkura daijin*, "the minister of finance," because they understand that the family budget is completely in her hands, and when they need money it would be pointless to raise the issue with anyone else. It is the woman of the house who is in control of family money matters, and she typically decides how much money is given over for spending by family members. Children and their fathers normally receive monthly spending allowances, referred to as *okozukai*. Although a very large purchase, perhaps an automobile, will be mulled over between a married couple for some time, everyday budgetary matters are in the wife's hands. Many Japanese men we know personally have only the vaguest notions of their savings and investment profiles, being content as is the normal pattern to let a wife handle money matters. When husbands and wives go together to Japan's new burgeoning supermarkets, as they both stand in line at the checkout counter, it is almost always the woman who hands over the payment.

As evidence of the dominant role Japanese women play in household finances, unlike just about anywhere else, stockbrokers sell door to door in Japan, understanding that it is the housewife who controls the budget for family investments. Interestingly, following the stock market crash in Japan in the early 1990s, many wives faced the unpleasant duty of informing their husbands that a large part of their family savings had been lost.

It isn't so much that men dominate women in Japan, but rather that men and women are more separated into *outside* and *inside* arenas of adult control. At work, the ideal is for men to play the role of the adults in authority; but inside the home, men, along with children, become dependents of women, who turn out in most cases to wear the mantle of real adult responsibility.

There is an irony surrounding the role of women in Japan, however. On the one hand, men expect women to be extremely feminine and completely nonthreatening in public. Female office workers take on almost infantile personalities in the workplace. Most women artificially raise their voices to extremely high pitches when talking to men at work; they understand that men prefer women to project childlike images, interpreted in Japan as cute and pleasant. In any group where men and women have to interact together in public, most women make a conspicuous point of deferring to men in regard to opinions and decisions.

As mothers and wives, on the other hand, women are expected to be paragons of strength and good judgment, and in that context men far more completely and readily defer to women than in the United States and other Western societies. Women bear the burden of running all the really important affairs of the family, almost as if their husbands had stored all responsibilities in lockers at work. If a Japanese man puts on too much weight, for instance, rather than placing blame on him, some people will end up criticizing his wife for overfeeding him. After all, it is her job to take care of things at home, and this includes the personal welfare and appearance of her husband.

Informal discussions among women, occasionally quite realistically reproduced in television dramas, reveal an underlying feeling that, along with the other duties of being a wife, women must bear the additional burden of "raising" their husbands. True, this idea is prevalent to some extent in the United States as well, but in Japan it goes a little further and seems to be more pervasive. Young men, after being pampered by their mothers as children, are not expected to be ready to take care of social responsibilities. Young males, considered to be inherently immature in their personal lives, are expected to be compelled toward maturity over time by the triple forces of school, employer, and wife. During the daytime, men are completely in charge of running the important affairs of Japan. But once they leave their jobs, these caretakers of the businesses and services of one of the most dynamic economies of our time tend to be seen by adult women as grown-up boys at play.

CONCLUSION

In religion, language, historical ties and other ways, the contrast between Japan and the United States is striking. In regard to life in the family, however, there are fewer differences between the two societies (although some remarkable ones do exist, particularly concerning male and female roles in marriage). This is because family type is greatly influenced by economic circumstances. The basic economic organization of a society determines what people do, which in turn influences the way society organizes itself to get these things done. For thousands of years, the form of economic organization most common in the world had been the agrarian political-economic system, and most people living in such societies were peasant farmers. It cannot be a coincidence that almost all of these societies developed a form of what sociologists call the extended family, a type of kinship organization that emphasizes vertical ties through the male line, and in which women leave their own lineage group and join that of husbands. Male dominance, prestige given to the elderly, marriage as a family matter rather than a personal, romantic relationship are some characteristics shared by extended families everywhere. Japan held onto that type of family structure much longer than the societies of Western Europe, which were in the process of changing to another type of family system as far back as 300 years ago. The family that has replaced the extended family in the modern world is the smaller nuclear family, which gives more primacy to a married couple. Japan did not begin to adopt the nuclear model until well into this century, and various aspects of the old system still influence ideas and behavior in various ways.

In the selection of wives and husbands in Japan, for example, older notions of family or, at least, parental oversight of the courtship process have not been completely swept away. A full one-third of Japanese still meet their future wife or husband through an omiai, an arranged meeting for the purpose of determining compatibility for marriage between two people who have never formally met before. Most Amercians would perhaps characterize relations between Japanese husbands and wives as being "taken for granted" rather than exhibiting the continuity of romantic love. Data concerning divorce and separation indicate that the Japanese family is more stable on average than in the United States. Certainly, Japanese married couples usually spend far less time together than those in other industrial societies, and some of the marriage stability is rooted in the extreme difficulty many women have in supporting themselves and their children after divorce.

The status of women in Japan is more complex than it appears from the outside. There is more obvious and pronounced ranking of men over women in the world outside the home than in any Western society, and symbols of that ranking are very easy to detect and are widely understood by non-Japanese. What is not so widely understood are the privileges of women in Japan. Since fewer Japanese married women work outside the home, they typically have more time for themselves than American women, and in some ways they have more power over domestic life than their counterparts in Europe or America. Women are more fully in charge of running the household in Japan and are usually in almost complete control of the household budget.

CHAPTER 8

Religion

While it is of course true that not all individuals are religious, religion is a universal feature of all human societies. As Émile Durkheim (1954) showed many years ago in his book *The Elementary Forms of the Religious Life*, societies have needs that can only be served by religion, and the interplay between religion and the rest of society has for a very long time been of great interest to sociologists. In addition to Durkheim, several of the great social theorists, especially Max Weber, paid special attention to the way religion both grew from specific social arrangements and affected the nature of some of those arrangements. Religion is certainly one of the most varied, complex, and fascinating of all human phenomena.

Most people who read these lines know of course that there are many forms of religious expression in the world. The range of most Americans' and Europeans' familiarity with religious expression, however, tends to be limited to religions that have historical ties and are therefore rather similar—Christianity, Judaism, Islam. Even a brief discussion of religious beliefs and practices in Japan offers a chance to go beyond this limited scope and begin to understand just how varied religious expression really is.

In this chapter we will examine the nature of religion in Japan, particularly the Shinto and Buddhist religions and the dual role they play in the Japanese society. We will also look at the problem of cults in Japan today; finally, we will discuss the extensive practices in magic and divination.

JAPANESE RELIGIONS

A casual visitor to Japan would likely conclude that it is a deeply religious place. Signs of religious practice and belief are everywhere, from large and well-maintained religious structures in the biggest cities to neighborhood shrines and temples; even in the deepest countryside one frequently comes across tiny altars and religious statues, in some cases relatively far from any dwelling or settlement. One of the first things a visitor to Japan is likely to notice is the architecture of Buddhist temples and Shinto shrines. They stand out so much because, in addition to being virtually everywhere Japanese people live, they usually are the only traditional buildings—the kind of physical evidence people who grow up in Western societies associate with Asia—still found in contemporary Japan. Costumes and rituals connected with the people who preside at these places are in some respects similar to scenes in other parts of Asia, but they are quite distinct from anything usually found in the West.

We recently read a travel brochure that described Japan as having two major religions, Buddhism and Shinto. Although true, that statement could be extremely misleading because it fails to point out a characteristic that sets Japan apart from the rest of the world. Normally, if a society has, say, two major religious orientations, people are associated with one or the other. If someone, for example, pointed out that two major religions of India are Hinduism and Islam, it would be accurate to imagine that the two religions have historically divided people into separate groups and that the two bodies have been rivals and even bitter enemies on occasion. But this is not the case in Japan: Buddhism and Shinto are not rival religions; people do not belong to one or the other. Individuals in Japan, actually over 95 percent of the adult population, have for well over 1,000 years embraced two completely separate religions at the same time, using one for some purposes, the other for other purposes.

Buddhism and Shinto both constitute what sociologists usually categorize as a **church.** The term signifies a religious tradition widely accepted as legitimate, with a considerable history and stable organizational and theological features. In Japan, these two religions have divided up religious chores. Shinto takes care of things like weddings, christenings, blessings for success in various enterprises, and a few others, whereas a main duty for Buddhism long ago evolved into taking care of the dead through funerals and memorials at certain intervals after death. Buddhism also has its own system of blessings and good-luck rituals. But even when the work of the two overlap, there has been a remarkable lack of any sense of competition between the two throughout Japanese history. Buddhist temples, *o-tera* in Japanese, and Shinto *jinja*, normally rendered into English as "shrines," are found in every neighborhood, attended at various times of the year by the same people. Today, temples and shrines are mostly supported by money donations given each year from local residents, and most receive enough funds for adequate maintenance and staffing. In many parts of rural Japan, the two religions share the same grounds, with both a temple and shrine standing side by side.

SHINTO

The Shinto religion is by far the older of the two. It is native to Japan and has only token representation in any other nation. Shinto grew out of a particular type of ancient nature worship and animism in which local spirits, usually identified with animals, together with physical objects in the landscape, were imbued with relative degrees of a type of supernatural power the Japanese call *kami*. An alternate reading of the Chinese character for kami is *shin*, and the label Shinto means simply the way of kami. Shinto has always been closely associated with the agricultural cycle, and even today the emperor, who plays the role of high priest of Shinto, transplants a few strands of rice sprouts in a Shinto ceremony each spring to symbolize the beginning of the rice-planting season.

There was a time when Shinto was elevated to the official national religion with government support and the imposition of a large organizational structure of ranked shrines throughout the nation. This began in the 1880s and 1890s and continued in various degrees right up to the end of World War II. The new leaders of Japan were desperate to form a strong national identification among all the Japanese people as the country ended its feudal period and opened its doors to the outside world (Gluck 1985). This was after the military ruler, the shogun, had been toppled from power in a relatively bloodless civil war that ended in 1868. For hundreds of years prior to that, individual identity for most Japanese had been as a member of a local fief under the head of a warlord. The men who came to power at that time were convinced that the nation needed to be tied tightly together with national institutions, such as the emperor, and a national religion in order to build a strong sense of identity for the state. Thus, the Shinto religion was sort of reinvented at that time into a complex network with official government sponsorship. Some new theology was hastily put together for Shinto, most of which was designed to instill pride of nation. Some of this new Shinto-based nationalism was openly racist and glorified Japan's acts of aggression and imperialism in Asia. Primarily for that reason, during the United States occupation of Japan following defeat in the war, national Shinto was completely dismantled and it went back to being what it was before the late nineteenth century, basically a community religious institution divided into very loose networks without sponsorship or financial help from the national government.

BUDDHISM

The Buddhist religion came to Japan from China during the period of intense borrowing of all things Chinese back in the fifth and sixth centuries AD. For a few hundred years, Buddhism stayed mainly a system of magic and blessing for the elite classes; in fact for a while it never got much outside the capital, first Nara, and later Kyoto when it became the capital in 794. Buddhism is a world religion, and there are certain overriding aspects of the faith that tie Japan very loosely with other Buddhist countries in East and Southeast Asia. Religion, however, has to fit into any society it is taken into, and as the Japanese are particularly good at domesticating foreign cultural imports, it was not long before a distinctly Japanese version of Buddhism began to develop. Although still mainly a religion for aristocrats, two branches of Buddhism were formed, one called *Tendai* and the other *Shingon*, the latter of which is still an important part of Japanese Buddhism today.

Slowly Buddhist teachings seeped into the lives of common people; by the tenth century, Buddhist temples could be found in all parts of Japan. In the twelfth and thirteenth centuries, three new popular Buddhist movements swept Japan: Pure Land Buddhism,

Nichiren Buddhism, and Zen. Formation of other branches of the religion and splintering off of older organizations has produced something like the case with Protestantism in Europe and the United States: many separate groups with subtle differences in theory and practice, but with no one group ever reaching a position of dominance over all the others. All the while, Shinto continued to be an important part of both official ceremony surrounding the emperor and the everyday affairs of ordinary people.

DEATH AND FUNERALS

As suggested above, the main duty of Buddhism, and frankly the source of most of its income, has centered on taking care of the dead. Funerals are the most prominent part of the Buddhist system of rituals, but taking care of the dead in Japan goes beyond simply performing funerals. After people die, a series of memorial services are held at various intervals; these must be performed by official ordained priests. The services begin for most branches of Buddhism in Japan 49 days following the funeral, then again at three years, seven years, and up to ten years, providing there are still family and friends around that long to arrange and pay for them.

In previous times, Japanese buried their dead; but for many decades now, all Japanese (except the emperor and his immediate family) by law must be cremated. A few days following death, the family and friends meet at the family temple to share a simple meal and reminisce over the life of the person whose funeral will be held the following day. In some cases the unembalmed body is viewed during this ceremony through a small window in the wooden box holding the body. It is still customary to provide a place at the table for the departed, signified with a bowl of rice with chopsticks stuck in from the top. The next day, with usually a somewhat larger group on hand, priests will begin the actual funeral ritual, which consists mainly of sutra chanting that continues for about an hour; the sutras are approximations of Sanskrit texts, and no one in the audience has any understanding of their meaning. During the chanting all participants in the funeral approach an altar and toss a small amount of incense into a large bowl. Following all the chanting and incense transfer, the entire party repairs to the crematorium to wait while the body goes through the actual cremation process. An hour or so later, family and friends pick small pieces of cooled, charred bones, with two people using separate pairs of chopsticks grabbing a single piece together and placing it in a special urn. The urn containing the remains is then either deposited in the family stone cemetery monument or placed in an honored space within the home of one of the survivors. (Two ritual ingredients of funeral rites, sticking a set of chopsticks into the center of a bowl of rice and people holding a single item at the same time with two sets of chopsticks, have become so associated with funerals that all children in Japan are taught never to engage in either of these two acts at the dinner table.)

With the exception of funerals and memorials after death, there has never been anything like mass, a sermon, or church service in Japan, in either of their religions. People relate to both religions mainly in a private way, by pausing at the altar of a temple or shrine and engaging in a very personal ritual of respect. There are, on the other hand, literally hundreds of festivals centering on both temples and shrines, with virtually every neighborhood in the land having its own festival of whatever size at an allotted time during the year. A few of these festivals, such as the Nebuta Festival in the city of Aomori in extreme northern Japan and the Hakata Dontaku in Fukuoka in northern Kyushu, have become popular tourist attractions for which millions of dollars are spent in preparation.

A little over 1 percent of Japanese are professed Christians. However, Christians in Japan have had more influence than their small numbers would suggest, and in the sixteenth century the Christian population reached as high as perhaps 5 percent. But in spite of intense work by thousands of dedicated foreign missionaries, the percentage of Christians has not increased appreciably over the past 100 years.

THE ROLE OF RELIGION IN JAPANESE LIFE

People whose ideas concerning religion are influenced by faiths most accessible in Europe and America—Christianity, Judaism, Islam—tend to see religion as the matrix of morality and good behavior. The term righteous, for example, can mean simply "very religious," or it can also mean "upright and moral" in a nonreligious sense. Historically, the two concepts have been closely linked in the Western mind. It must be surprising then for people from Western

TABLE 8-1

The Importance of Religion

Country	% Believe in a God	Importance of Religion in Life (10-point scale)
United States	98%	8.55
Ireland	97	8.02
Spain	92	6.39
Italy	88	6.96
England	81	5.72
Germany (West)	80	5.67
France	65	4.72
Japan	62	4.49

Source: *The Gallup Report,* May 1985, p. 52; World Values Survey, Shapiro (1992), p. 40.

tradition to hear that in Japan there is little if any link between religion and morality, ethics, or standards of right behavior. This must be especially puzzling in light of the amazingly low rate of crime in modern Japan. If you think that a society must use religion to keep people in line, well, Japan proves you are wrong. Japanese society is very orderly, but social order in Japan stems mostly from obligations to people as described in Chapter 2, not from religion.

Even a brief description of religion in Japan would not be complete without mentioning something of the extremely modest role religion actually plays in the mental life of the average Japanese person, as indicated in Table 8–1. There are two overriding characteristics of religion in Japan that seem to be polar opposites but nonetheless are both true. On the one hand, Japanese are as loyal to the rituals of their traditional religions as any people in the world. On the other hand, a large portion of these same people, who would never think of failing to visit a temple or shrine during one of the three days of the New Year's celebration (January 1, 2, or 3 of each year), label themselves *mushinsha,* literally "nonbeliever."

The kind of emotional engagement and deep commitment one often sees among religious people in other societies is to a great degree absent in the religious life of Japan. There is very little that is analogous to devoting one's life to God, Jesus, or Allah in the Japanese experience. Even the clergy in Japan relate to their work more like technicians than as guides to some deep spiritual truth. Priests in Japan provide services that are needed for various events; they learn how to apply the rituals and operate the ceremonies. In their personal lives they are, and are expected to be, people with attitudes, lifestyles, and personal habits undistinguished from anyone else. Japanese don't invite members of the clergy into their homes for dinner the way Americans often do. But if they did, they would likely treat the person like any other guest, without a sense that language and manners should be carefully controlled in the presence of one with a special holy calling.

In fact, measured by amount of religious activity—such as attending church, believing in a god, believing in an afterlife, or simply asking people how important religion is in their lives— Japanese people are among the least religious people in major industrial societies. Various *Gallup Reports* have shown that people in the United States are among the most religious in the world (usually Ireland is slightly ahead), whereas Japanese people are among the least. It is far from a perfect analogy, but most Japanese relate to religion as Westerners do to the celebration of Halloween. Halloween has survived through many centuries and shows little sign of dying out. Generation after generation of Americans and Europeans recognize Halloween in various and changing ways; it's something people participate in because of tradition and because it can be fun. But it certainly is not something anyone would think of as a major focus of life, or even something to take very seriously at all. Although religion is certainly more pervasive and important in Japan than Halloween is in the West, in both cases the degree of typical individual psychological commitment is similar.

SECTS AND CULTS IN JAPAN TODAY

A **sect** is defined as a type of religious group that stands out somewhat from the rest in that its religious practices have broken away from those of established churches and run counter in some way to the traditions of a given society. It is as a sect, of course, that most major world religions began, which includes Christianity, the original Indian Buddhism, and the various branches of Japanese Buddhism. Contemporary Japan, just as most modern nations, has been the birthplace of many new religious movements over the past several centuries, though most have either died out or remained relatively small on the national religious map. During the past few decades, some, while not very strong in numbers, have displayed an impressive facility for raising money and persuading devotees to turn over their property to the organization, in the process accumulating hundreds of millions of dollars in assets.

One sect in particular grew in the postwar period to achieve the status of a major religious organization with ties to an important political party. This sect is called *Sōka Gakkai*, "value creating association" in Japanese, while abroad it is often known as *Nichiren Shoshu*, reflecting its self-styled association to Nichiren, a well-known theologian of the thirteenth century. Sōka Gakkai encourages much more emotional involvement in religion than ordinary Buddhism or Shinto, and in the 1950s it dramatically expanded, even forming its own political party, the *Kōmeitō*, or "clean government party." The growth curve of Sōka Gakkai eventually slowed and even stopped, but although ties between the religious body and political party have been officially banned as unconstitutional, it remains a powerful organization with just under 10 percent of the religious affiliation of the nation.

A **cult** is a sectlike group that harbors beliefs and follows practices even less widely accepted by the society at large. Because of the controversial character of their beliefs and practices, cult members tend to be isolated from the rest of society, and in some cases the isolation involves complete physical separation. Isolated as they are, cult members are vulnerable to extremist ideas and often come to have complete faith in a charismatic leader, no matter how strange his or her ideas might seem to an outsider. We cannot leave this discussion of religion in Japan without mentioning something about one of the most spectacular cults to emerge anywhere in the twentieth century.

The Aum Shinrikyō

Japan is a relatively orderly and dependable place. It has, for example, the lowest crime rate of any of the larger industrial nations; in recent history, people there have gone about their daily business without any need to fear an encounter with anyone or anything that could harm them in any way. The country has its share of calamities, but these are almost always brought on by nature—things like typhoons, earthquakes, and droughts. Citizens of Japan have traditionally tended to feel that as long as they stayed home, that is to say, in Japan, they would be able to trust the people and institutions around them to keep them safe and protected.

That rather remarkable sense of security in the routines of ordinary life was suddenly shattered, at least temporarily, on March 20, 1995, when small bottles of the deadly gas sarin were released simultaneously in cars on three of Tokyo's busiest subway lines during rush hour. Only 11 people were killed, but over 5,000 were injured enough to require medical treatment. A month and a half later, on May 5, two canisters of highly poisonous cyanide gas attached to a timing device were discovered and disarmed by security forces in a toilet area of Shinjuku station, gateway to the western suburbs of Tokyo and one of the busiest train stations in the world. Police investigators estimated that there was enough cyanide in the canisters to kill at least 10,000 people. Stunned, and initially baffled, authorities slowly began to trace the two incidents to a religious cult called *Aum Shinrikyō*. (*Shinrikyō* translates to something like, "true knowledge," or "true way." *Aum* is a sound used in Hindu and Tibetan Buddhist chanting and usually spelled "oum" in English.)

The Aum Shinrikyō cult had membership of less than 5,000 people in Japan, only a few hundred of whom were full-time, live-in devotees, and a few hundred more in, of all places, Russia. It was founded by an enigmatic figure who called himself Shoko Asahara, a brilliant student while in university and a person with a highly charismatic personality. Like more than a dozen such groups that have sprung up in Japan over the past 50 years, Aum Shinrikyō was highly secretive and demanded complete devotion from followers. What set Aum Shinrikyō apart from the others was its ability to attract highly educated people with technical skills, in some cases graduates from the most prestigious universities in the country.

A few followers of the cult eventually cooperated with police, and the stories they told were utterly fantastic, sounding more like the scenario from a James Bond movie than anything in real life. Some former members told of bizarre schemes to bomb Tokyo with lethal gas, killing most of its population and holding the rest of the country hostage in order to actually take control of the nation. Not all of the allegations were proved, but it was discovered that the cult had a large poison gas factory at the foot of Mt. Fuji and that automatic weapons were being manufactured there. It also came to light that more than 20 people were murdered by the cult, including a lawyer trying to help parents retrieve children from the cult, and 7 additional people were killed the previous June in a rural area as the cult practiced releasing poison gas.

The arrest and trial of Shoko Asahara and the other leaders of the cult mesmerized the nation, receiving higher television ratings than even the death and funeral of Emperor Hirohito in 1989. Never has a man been hated by so many Japanese.

People in Japan are certainly not alone in their occasional vulnerability to making dramatic commitments to groups promising emotional fulfillment and the achievement of some lofty purpose. Cults have been part of the life of all modern societies in recent decades as well as throughout history. And we must remind ourselves that as dangerous as Aum Shinrikyō appeared to be, a few thousand individuals is a very tiny representation of the Japanese population. It is true, on the other hand, that standard religious practices in Japan offer very little sense of any purpose or meaning; hence, some people see commitment to some sort of extremist cause, be it a political or quasi-religious movement, as the only available outlet for devotion. It is therefore not surprising that, although small in numbers of members, there are about 1,500 religious sects or cults with headquarters at the foot of Mt. Fuji alone.

MAGIC AND DIVINATION IN CONTEMPORARY JAPAN

A foreigner from a Western society cannot live in Japan for long without realizing that there is more popular magic and **divination** around in everyday life than he or she is used to at home. Parts of all societies incorporate magical practices both within and outside of established religion to attempt to influence the outcome of events beyond human control. The yearning to understand and control events is a major reason religious practices develop in human societies. Praying, for example, from a strictly technical standpoint is a sort of applied magic when it involves asking for something to happen or not to happen.

Attitudes toward divination and fortune-telling in Japan differ significantly from those in most Western countries. In the United

States, for example, it was something of a minor scandal when it was revealed that while living in the White House from 1981 until 1989, Nancy Reagan routinely consulted an astrologer, with the implication that some of what the astrologer told her could have affected decisions made by her husband, the president. It would be difficult to imagine something like that causing so much negative attention in Japan. Regular sessions with fortune-tellers is so common for people of all walks of life in Japan that it would be unusual to find that someone making an important decision had *not* consulted one, including the executives of Japan's biggest corporations.

In the West, the Church in the Middle Ages incorporated some aspects of popular magic and banned all other forms of magic and divination as the work of the devil. Even today, the amount of nonreligious magic and divination practiced by average people in Western societies is limited to just a few forms, astrology being the most popular. The Japanese never experienced a similar purge of popular magic and divination, so as one might imagine, there are more forms of them around for everyone to see, and they play a more prominent role in the lives of people in Japan than in other industrial societies.

Currently, the Japanese use the same Gregorian monthly calendar as that used in all modern societies. Many of the calendars hanging in homes and offices all over Japan include categorizations of each day of every month as "very propitious" (a good day for marriages and other important events), "somewhat propitious" (OK for some important events), or "impropitious" (a bad day to plan events). Wedding halls are very expensive to rent on propitious days, and although those halls could be rented at a fraction of that cost on impropitious days, there are few takers.

Hardly a single building is ever erected in Japan, from office buildings to private residences to warehouses, without first consulting a system of geomancy, divination that establishes the most favorable place for entrances, toilets, kitchens, and other features of the structure. This kind of divination, along with many other aids in reaching decisions, is not officially part of Buddhism or Shinto. It is part of a multibillion dollar industry that relies on private practitioners who study and practice as sort of divination counselors.

The percentage of people in Japan who consult fortune-tellers is significantly higher than in other industrial societies. It would be difficult to come up with an exact figure—Japanese have come to be a

Most Japanese homes have a butsudan, *or Buddhist alter, located in one of the main rooms. It is made of black lacquer and gold leaf like the one in the photograph. Ashes of dead parents or grandparents are sometimes stored here and small amounts of food are periodically left on the shelf as a symbolic offering to the departed.*

bit sensitive about reporting their involvement with various forms of divination—but a good indication can be had by comparing the advertisements for fortune-telling services in the telephone directories of major cities. Several entries advertise fortune-telling services in the Los Angeles yellow pages, taking up about a quarter of a page. In Tokyo, however, the yellow pages of the telephone directory currently list 440 fortune-telling establishments, including a few half-page ads, and the entire section of fortune-telling ads runs on for nine pages. Even all the people who pay for the ads in the telephone directory represent only a segment of the fortune-telling population. Several times that many are part-time fortune-tellers who do not advertise publicly for fear of attracting the attention of Japan's national income tax authorities.

CONCLUSION

Although religions fulfill certain social needs, needs that are generally similar throughout the world, the way they do so differs across societies. Westerners are used to a single, all-powerful God; to the notion that religions are exclusive, that a person can be associated with only one at a time; and to the idea of religious ethics and commandments. None of these things are part of the religion of the overwhelming majority of the Japanese people. There is no monotheistic God in Japan; people there have more than one religious affiliation; and in spite of Japan being a relatively orderly and crime-free nation, religions there don't have much to say about behavior. Ethics in Japan do not necessarily flow from religious teachings; rather, it is from a sense of obligation to others that Japanese ethics derive, a purely secular system of social control.

Most people in the world belong to a particular religious tradition. However, in Japan all but a tiny minority of Christians and others practice two religions at the same time, using each for specific purposes. The two religions are Shinto, the native religion of Japan, and Buddhism, which was brought to Japan more than 1,000 years ago. Shinto is a kind of modernized animism, with various local spirits and deities; the idea is that even inanimate objects can possess a type of divine power called kami. Shinto specializes in initiating things: blessing of new buildings and businesses, christening of babies, and performing the actual wedding ceremony prior to the

Although Japanese in some ways are not very religious, few fail to visit an o-tera *or* jinja *during the three days of New Year's celebration.*

large and public wedding banquet. Buddhism specializes in dealing with death and the departed, from funerals to memorial services long after death.

The past two centuries have witnessed the birth of several new religions in Japan, and as is usually the case, these began as sects, or new organizations outside the traditional religious framework. An example of a sect that eventually gained considerable following, great wealth, and even considerable political power in Japan is Sōka Gakkai, with several million adherents. Japan is also the home of cults and cultlike religious organizations, groups with secret and occasional antisocial leanings. One of the most dramatic revelations of cult activity anywhere in the world followed the recent poison gas attack on Tokyo subway lines by the Aum Shinrikyō, a group whose methods and goals are so strange and deadly that they are almost beyond belief.

Magic and divination play a much more prominent and public role in Japan than in other modern societies. Fortune-telling and forms of divination such as geomancy are the focus of multibillion dollar industries.

CHAPTER 9

Education

Education, together with family, religion, the military, formal governance, and a few others, are normally counted among what sociologists call **social institutions**—those fairly standardized areas of organized effort that handle the main tasks of a society. However, as a large, professionally organized system with relatively standardized goals and techniques, formal education really hasn't been around that long in the span of human history. Until a little over 100 years ago, the great majority of people on earth had never stepped foot inside a school. Unlike religion, which all known societies have always had, school systems for ordinary people are part of only the modern world; in fact, the modernization of any society can be measured by the extent and quality of its system of mass education. The United States was one of the first nations to realize the advantage of mass education, and as it developed first primary school systems, then secondary education, and finally a system of higher education available to large segments of the population, rapid and impressive economic development quickly followed, although schooling was not the sole reason.

The rather sudden bursting on the scene of post–World War II Japan as first an industrial success story, and then far more than that, as a true economic superpower, has focused much attention on the nature of Japanese society and institutions. People everywhere are naturally curious as to just how Japan was able to grow in industrial power so rapidly. As the world discovered that Japan routinely leads the world in many subjects on achievement tests given to school children, while American school children consistently rank toward the bottom, a great deal of interest has been drawn to education as one of Japan's great strengths. Certainly, in terms of factual information and basic technical learning provided, it is difficult to find a system available to the mass of people on the primary and secondary school levels that matches Japan's in quality, reminiscent of the way the United States led the world in quality secondary education a century before.

There are many facets to the educational environment in Japan that are worthy of note, but in spite of the impressive results mentioned above, not all of them are particularly flattering. Long ago, foreign observers noticed an almost fanatical devotion to study by a large portion of Japanese school-age children. In addition, parents, or at least mothers, often get avidly involved in the academic progress of their children, something universally touted by American experts as the most important single ingredient in continued success for children at school; but at times such involvement can be excessive. Also, there is the overriding importance of entrance examinations at various levels of progress through the system, initially for entrance into high schools and later to qualify for universities. As we shall see, these examinations produce an enormous amount of stress in the lives of young people in Japan.

In this chapter we will consider the nature of the Japanese educational system, how it developed and how it is in many ways different from that of the United States today. We will describe the extreme competitiveness of the educational system and how most successful students must go to special after-hours schools, usually called *juku*. Finally, we will look at the Japanese university system and how it differs from the American university system.

THE JAPANESE EDUCATIONAL SYSTEM

Americans will find some aspects of education in Japan more familiar than systems in most other parts of the world. A diagram of the school system reveals a structure similar in most ways to the traditional structure common in the United States since the late 1930s. That structure—kindergarten followed by six years of elementary schooling, three years of junior high school, and three years of senior high school—was set in place by the education mission of the U.S. occupation authority immediately following World War II. When the formal U.S. occupation ended in 1952, Japan was free to return to its earlier and quite different structure, but it chose to keep the American pattern and in fact has been more loyal to that one pattern than school districts across the United States.

Another similarity in the educational dimensions of the two societies is the very high percentage of high school graduates who attend college—just slightly under half of all college-age people are students in higher education in both societies. Europe and other Asian societies normally have much lower percentages, typically 10 to 20 percent.

However, as is the case with family life and many other aspects of life in the two societies, although the education systems may look similar on the surface, when we look more closely at how they actually work, differences immediately arise and quickly become more impressive than similarities. Table 9–1 lists a few of the interesting differences between Japan, the United States, and some other countries with respect to matters related to education.

TABLE 9-1

Comparative Education Figures

Country	School Days per Year	College Attendance*	School Effectiveness**	Science Test Scores†
Japan	243	35.3%	75.5	20.2
Germany	210	28.1	75.2	—
Netherlands	200	—	64.6	19.8
France	185	28.6	49.7	—
England	192	20.9	40.6	16.7
United States	180	45.7	47.6	16.5

* Among college-age young people.
**Effectiveness rating for economic competitiveness (top ranking 100) by Swiss "World Competitiveness Report."
† Test scores of 14-year-olds on standard science test.
Source: Keizai Koho (1995); Shapiro (1992), pp. 58, 60, 66.

In Japan, formal required schooling only extends to the end of junior high school by law; in theory, high school attendance is strictly optional. But, because schooling in Japan has come since the 1950s to be so closely linked to the type of job a person can get, almost all Japanese of both sexes, 97 percent in fact, complete high school even though it is not compulsory.

One enters high school in Japan by passing an entrance examination. About 20 percent of high schools are industrial high schools (Rohlen 1983), or what Americans would call vocational schools emphasizing practical training for jobs. The examinations for entrance into those kinds of high schools are rather easy, but going to a vocational high schools does not prepare a young man or woman to pass the examination for a university or college. One of the important functions of counselors in junior high school is to guide students toward which high school they have the most realistic chance of getting in. We should add here that vocational high schools in Japan are not mere warehouses for dumb students as is regrettably the case in many American school districts. Vocational schools in Japan offer high quality training with up-to-date equipment donated by industry. Most of these schools are for males only, and their graduates are well qualified for work in many industries. They are literate, know basic science, and have mathematics skills characteristic of only a small portion of American high school graduates. Strong ties between these vocational schools and particular corporations provide a strong incentive for the students to work hard to land the best jobs (Rosenbaum and Kariya 1989).

Certainly, separate academic and vocational high schools is not the most dramatic difference between education in Japan and the United States. The biggest single difference is in what happens to the majority of high school students, the ones who go to schools that have the kind of curricula necessary for preparing for the entrance examinations for colleges and universities. Most of you would have a hard time imagining the intensity of the ordeal these students go through. If the act of studying from books could be converted into electrical power, surely Japan would be the best lit place on earth. Every society has its share of bookworms; students with good study habits are not confined to any one country or part of the world. It is quite likely, however, that young Japanese who aim to attend a reputable university, probably 70 or 80 percent of the student body of academic high schools, spend more hours of serious academic study on average than high-school-age people of any other society.

THE IMPORTANCE OF EDUCATION IN JAPAN

The reason they study so hard is rooted in the role higher education plays in Japan. In Japan, higher education is used in a very direct way to identify, at a very early age, leadership for the most powerful organizations in the nation. For those who attend the most reputable institutions of higher education, status and opportunities will be available that others will not experience. That may sound strange. After all, in most societies opportunities for success are limited without credentials earned in higher education. So what is different about Japan? It's a little difficult to adequately explain in such short space, but what makes the Japanese system different is that so much is funneled into a narrow selection process with hardly any alternatives or exceptions. Even the sons and daughters of wealthy and successful Japanese will have a difficult time retaining upper-middle-class status and standards without traveling that one narrow path.

If we take a wide look at the United States by comparison the difference becomes clearer. Of course, it helps to go to a reputable university for a chance at almost any successful career. Life in the United States, however, has lots of little bypaths and second opportunities; so one cannot always predict how successful a particular teenager will be. Success in a U.S. organization is most often determined during one's working career, dependent on how well the individual works with situations and people. Americans often go back to college for advanced degrees, which can bring great rewards under the right conditions. In Japan, most of the determinants of success—certainly at the top of the social system—are wrapped up in one afternoon when a person is 18 years old. It is the afternoon one sits for the examination for entrance into the university.

What actually drives the system of selection for success in Japan is something the Japanese call *gakureki*, which translates literally to "education record," but it means much more than that. Gakureki refers to a system of selection and reward in the most strategic areas of society, those things we think of as representing the highest level of individual success, based almost solely on the rank of the university one has attended—not on grades earned at college, not on distinctions of any kind earned while there, just the fact that one attended that particular institution. As explained in more detail below, Japanese universities are easy to get through; in fact, graduation is virtually guaranteed in four years whether one studies hard or not. Just getting in, then, is all that really matters; but getting in at a top-ranked university requires an unbelievable amount of intense preparation. It needs to be pointed out that Japanese universities, at least the top 15 or 20, the ones that really count, are part of a widely agreed-upon ranking. Americans recognize the high ranking of Harvard and the University of California, Berkeley as among the best institutions in the country, but not everyone would list them as the top two, and beyond that there is only a broad category of top schools ranked differently by different people for different reasons. In Japan the top 10 or so institutions are pretty much in the same order in everyone's mind.

If a student can get into one of the top five or six, he (perhaps even she, if she is willing to run the risk of sacrificing the chance for normal Japanese marriage and family life) will be virtually guaranteed of what is considered in Japan to be an elite career, that is, a secure job with a top corporation or public agency offering much more prestige and usually higher pay than people who graduate from lesser institutions can achieve. If he (again, perhaps she) is somehow one of those few hundred walking encyclopedias who each year pass the exam for the one institution at the pinnacle of Japan's education pyramid, the University of Tokyo, the payoff is not merely an elite career; it is the real opportunity for leadership status in whatever organization the person blesses with his (her) presence. Graduates from the University of Tokyo, Todai as the Japanese call it, dominate at the top in every important part of Japanese life. For example, there have been 22 prime ministers since the end of World War II; 10 have been Todai graduates, and all 10 came from the same department, the Law Department of Todai. (Law in Japan is an undergraduate major concerned mainly with business law.) One recent study of the top three executive officers of the 75 largest corporations and banks in Japan found that 60 percent were Todai graduates (Kerbo and McKinstry 1995). By comparison, only a bit more than 10 percent of board members of the largest 250 corporations in the United States are graduates of Harvard, Yale, or Princeton. Is it any wonder then that the scramble to enter the top universities in Japan is so ferocious? If you pass the entrance exam for Todai, your chance of success is not merely good; it is just about guaranteed.

Scores on the examinations are not merely the most important determinant of who gets in; they are the *only* determinant. Extracurricular activities, athletic prowess, the stature and accomplishments of one's parents, even high school grades, all have no bearing at all on who gets into a university. Students take the examinations anonymously, identified to readers of the examinations by assigned number only, and they either pass or fail; that's it. The taking of the entrance examinations each spring by young Japanese who want to enter colleges and universities, *juken* as it is called in Japanese, has reached the level of national obsession. It is the subject of an endless number of newspaper stories and magazine articles, many featuring questions from past exams, and one of the most frequent topics of conversation, especially among college hopefuls.

The set of ideas that support gakureki were put in place in the latter part of the nineteenth century, soon after Japan threw off its system of hereditary selection of leaders (Gluck 1985). Officials of the new regime wanted young men trained in the ways of the Western world, but they were not ready to include ordinary people in a system of preparation for leadership. Early modern higher education in Japan was for the children of the former hereditary elite. At that time there was no higher secondary school system, and while theoretically anyone could take and pass the entrance examinations, only the elite class could afford the special tutoring required to prepare for them. Except for a few random geniuses from farm or worker families, early in the twentieth century university students were more often the products of well-to-do families. Gradually secondary schools spread across the country, and by the 1920s, people from all walks of life were receiving the kinds of preparatory education that made them realistic candidates for passing university entrance examinations. Slowly Japan began to replace its hereditary elite with one based more on academic merit, or at least a kind of merit inherent in memorizing huge amounts of factual material appropriate for passing entrance examinations to reputable universities. In Japan a general mind-set about people in leadership roles developed early, which largely still exists: that those people are naturally the graduates of a few elite universities and, further, that they are inherently superior to everyone else.

As you read this you are probably thinking that gakureki does not make a lot of sense. Imagine in the United States a tradition of unofficially reserving half of all top government and business positions to, say, graduates of Harvard. Waste of mountains of talent from other sources is only the most obvious weakness in such a system. The Japanese themselves seem to be very much aware of the self-imposed burden represented by gakureki. Although a great deal of criticism of gakureki appears throughout the country, including much talk about somehow doing away with it, there does not seem to be any way for an acceptable alternative to develop; hence the system is still very much alive in contemporary Japan.

AFTER-HOURS SCHOOLS: JUKU

If passing the entrance examinations to a good university is the only route to the most highly honored success, it is not hard to understand why focus on these examinations has spilled over from the ordinary school system into a system of private schools that supplement the regular curriculum and help the students bone up for the exams. These private schools are called *juku;* they range in size and formality from being not real schools at all but rather a room in someone's home where some private tutoring is carried out, to elaborate plants actually bigger than some public schools. More than half of all senior high school students in Japan, a good portion of junior high students, and even some elementary school pupils attend juku, some for two evenings a week plus Saturday afternoon (Japanese have regular school on Saturday morning, and the Saturday juku session follows three and a half hours of ordinary school), and a sizable minority attend some kind of juku class every single day of the week (Rohlen 1983; Stevenson and Baker 1992). Juku are not inexpensive, and they are not much fun; none that we know of offer any recreation or social functions of any kind. They are pure academic grind.

Some students who take and fail to pass the examination to the university they want to enter will sort of drop out of society, studying virtually all their waking hours for the entire year until the time for the next examination in the following spring. These students are called *rōnin*, the word used in feudal Japan to identify samurai without any clan to fight for, homeless warriors of a sort. Today, rōnin are school-less students. Academic rōnin commonly live in small apartments near the university they will try for again; they usually have little social life, spending virtually every day and most evenings studying in the university library.

That kind of pressure on a certain percentage of Japanese pre-college youth takes its toll. Many Japanese study so hard that they fail to develop social skills and ways of coping with the world outside the home typical of people their age in other societies. Each year literally tens of thousands of elementary and secondary school-age children acquire a neurotic symptom the Japanese call *tōkō kyohi*, literally "refusal to attend school." It is not that they are terrified of the school itself or of the people there; Japanese school teachers at all levels together with all other school personnel seem to be among the kindest and most patient people anywhere. That kind of neurosis is the only way some young Japanese imagine they can escape the intense pressure of gakureki.

Pressure to succeed in entering a reputable university has moved during the past 40 years or so backward down the age ladder, so that it really begins to build unbelievably early for young children. Many Japanese mothers now put their three- or four-year-olds through early tutoring to give them a better chance to qualify for special preschools, which they believe will get the children started on the long road to a highly ranked college.

JAPANESE UNIVERSITIES

A higher percentage of Japanese graduate from colleges and universities than Americans do, about 38 percent versus about 24 percent. However, it would not lead to a fair comparative assessment of higher education in the two societies if we let the above statement stand at that. In Japan, most of the academic intensity comes to a screeching halt the minute a person passes the entrance examination and begins life as a college student (Kerbo 1994). To put it bluntly, most Japanese students of even the best universities do not learn very much at college. With a few exceptions such as those in programs in engineering at selected universities, Japanese undergraduates (very few go on to graduate school) have a rather easy time of it. Curricula are not very demanding; most classes run for a full year in Japan from early April to the next March, but they have only one 90-minute meeting per week, which results in about 35 hours for each class for the entire year. Compare that to your classes, which normally meet for more than 40 hours each in a single semester; and although Japanese university students generally enroll in more classes in a given year than a typical American student, they actually need count only about the same number of classes as American students in order to move to the next year's level. It's no wonder that Japanese students usually enter universities fresh out of high school, rarely transfer to other institutions (if they did, they would have to start over as freshmen), and stay in lockstep order—freshman, sophomore, junior, senior in yearly succession—almost always graduating in exactly four years. You see then that there is some relief to the severe demands of student life in the Japanese system.

The average Japanese of precollege age is perfectly aware that he or she is not likely to join the gakureki elite. About half of graduating seniors actually go to college. Most end up in private institutions, only a few of which have rankings high enough to give them special advantages. Speaking bluntly once more, we should point out that most of the private, nonelite universities in Japan deserve their reputation of mediocrity. Even at the elite schools most students don't take academic life very seriously, as we have already pointed out. Nonelite higher education in Japan suffers the added burden of very poor ratios of students to faculty, resulting in huge class size of often hundreds of students. If there is any serious learning going on in most Japanese university classes (except for engineering and some other applied subjects), the Japanese are very good at concealing it. Most professors seem to sort of go through the motions of teaching, often delivering what American students would consider numbingly boring material, and student attendance is quite low and interest in class work minimal. Grades (which are always passing) are frequently based on written reports, something like take-home exams, which are often so general and undemanding as to actually insult the intelligence and academic background of the students.

Until the recession of the mid-1990s, these graduates from nondistinct private colleges and universities were able to get white-collar jobs in the corporate world with companies below the level of the elite track. Recently the Japanese have had to follow the pattern in other industrial nations of reducing the number of salaried employees to economize during difficult times, and it has become more difficult for graduates of nonelite institutions to land good jobs.

Research carried on by university faculty does not play as important a role in the development of technology in Japan as it does in other nations. Although some technological breakthroughs have occurred in university laboratories, most research and development that ends up helping Japanese industry is done by the corporations themselves.

Education in Japan, then, although it has served the country well and is in many ways the envy of the world, is not without its problems. Japan has one of the highest literacy rates in the world in spite of a writing system that is certainly among the world's most difficult to master. If we stopped random passers-by on the street in Japan and the United States, the Japanese would be far more likely to be able to solve a simple algebra problem than the American counterpart, and it is hard to see how that is anything but directly related to a higher quality of preparatory education.

CONCLUSION

There are several features of the education systems in Japan and the United States that set them apart from those of most other societies in the world. Both have the same basic structure: a year or so of kindergarten, six years of primary school, three years of junior high school, and three years of senior high school, followed by four years of college. The United States and Japan send higher percentages of their young people through their systems of higher education than other major nations. In examining the total picture, however, there are many more significant differences than similarities between the education systems of the two societies.

It is extremely difficult to succeed in Japan without proper educational credentials. A system the Japanese call gakureki has evolved that ranks the top 10 or 15 universities. As is the case everywhere, in Japan one's value as an employee is closely linked to university attendance, but even more to the rank of the university attended. University attendance is determined solely through entrance examinations, and the examinations to highly ranked universities are extremely difficult, requiring years of preparation. Enormous pressure mounts for ambitious young people in Japan to pass the examinations for entrance into the top universities, pressure that has worked its way down the age categories all the way to preschool. At the top of the university pyramid is the University of Tokyo. Roughly 40 percent of top political and business personnel are graduates of that institution, and the great majority of those come from one academic department, the Law Department. An auxiliary private system of after-hours schooling known as *juku* began to spread across Japan in the 1950s, and today nearly half of all Japanese attend juku during primary or secondary school ages. Perhaps 10 to 15 percent of people who take and fail entrance examinations become study hermits, spending nearly all waking hours preparing for the next round of exams given each spring.

It may surprise American students to learn that once in the university, most Japanese students really don't study very hard, and indeed that universities in Japan are not centers of learning and research to the extent they are in the United States. Universities in Japan are places where students develop lifelong friendships and learn social skills they haven't had time for in the long, arduous path into university life.

CHAPTER 10

Cities

As pioneering American sociologists at the University of Chicago showed us many years ago, when examining any modern society it is necessary to understand something of the nature of its major cities. The fruits and the failures of civilizations are often housed in urban centers. As long as cities have existed they have been at the heart of every civilized tradition. In fact, what we call civilization was originally spawned in the first urban places 7,000 years ago. When food-producing technology finally reached a point where not everyone had to be a producer, then craftsmen, traders, and even people who spent their time looking at the heavens congregated together in the first towns. It was there that a new intensity of the exchange of information and ideas was set into place that lifted humankind to levels unimagined before. It is possible to point to important events in human development not directly related to urban life: The great religions of Judaism and Islam grew originally from experiences of tribal people who lived at least part of the time in deserts, and pastoral references and attitudes are liberally expressed in the early literature of those religions. But had neither of those religions been eventually grafted onto urban-based societies, we would scarcely know of them today.

Perhaps to some foreign businesspeople who confine their experiences in Japan to the business districts of major cities, Japanese cities don't seem very different from those the world over. Of course the Japanese have adopted the international architecture for their large, modern buildings, and if you don't look too closely, and you don't go too far, while strolling around the downtown section of a Japanese city you'll see a lot of familiar images. However, as discussed in this chapter, historically, sociologically, and ecologically there is definitely something we could call the "Japanese city." We will consider first the Japanese attitude toward urban life, then some of the important characteristics and history of Japanese cities.

JAPANESE VIEWS OF THE CITY

The Japanese have for a very long time been especially attracted to urban life. Although it could be said that Japan got a rather late start in having cities—Nara, the first urban center did not begin to take shape until the middle of the eighth century—during most of recorded history the Japanese have strongly preferred urban over rural life, and for a long time, for the elite Kyoto-based population, banishment from the capital was among the severest of punishments. Even today, the term *inaka*, "country" or "countryside," draws up images in the Japanese mind of crudeness, backwardness, and simplicity in a distinctly negative sense. *Inakapei*, "bumpkin," is a person of the country, someone ignorant of the finer nuances of cultivated living. Of course *bumpkin* is an English word and occasionally still used in much that same way wherever English is spoken. In the English-speaking world, however, the idea of the countryside as outside the boundaries of civilization also suggests other more positive images: the gentleman farmer, for example, or the country residence of the British aristocracy. In the new world, men like Washington and Jefferson considered their true residence to be the country, not the city. In fact, one theme running through American history is that cities are evil places and the theories of those pioneering sociologists at the University of Chicago mentioned above incorporated a good deal of negative bias toward the city. Thus, whereas the idea of "country living" has traditionally had mixed associations, partly negative, partly positive, in most Western societies, this has not been so in Japan. Although Japan still has a slightly higher percentage of people who actually live in the countryside than the United States or England, the image of country living in Japan has for a very long time been overwhelmingly negative.

A major reason for low regard of the countryside in Japan is not difficult to understand. Until very recently there were only two kinds of cities in Japanese tradition. Kyoto originally was a fully planned city. It was the capital of Japan until the last century, the seat of the imperial court, the place where translated Chinese civilization was brought first and where the Japanese version of that civilization began to take root. All other traditional cities in Japan grew from castle towns in the medieval period. For most of the past 1,500 years, political authority in Japan was regional authority emanating from military rulers who lived in castles. Civil war raged over the land for almost 300 years until late in the seventeenth century. The areas around castles were the only places secure enough for sustained market activity, and for that reason all castles developed towns around them, the largest and most important ones eventually growing into true cities. European castles sometimes led to similar development, but in most cases castles in Europe and elsewhere did not form the nucleus of urban life. In Japan, however, urbanism and elite populations, with all that elitism comes to mean, were forged together. There never has been anything like a "country gentlemen" tradition in Japan, nothing to counter the image of the countryside as a place outside the orbit of the sophisticated, the refined, the admirable.

It is true that a phenomenon the Japanese call *u-turn* (English words and phrases are used frequently in Japan, although they are often used and pronounced differently from what English-speaking people would expect) has caught the attention of the media to a considerable extent for the past few years. A u-turn is when a person whose parents or grandparents moved from the country to the city in the past decides to escape the pressures of the city and return to the countryside, perhaps farming on leased land somewhere or pursuing some form of salable art or craft, such as pottery making, from a country cabin. Typically, the u-turner is a former white-collar employee of a large corporation. Interviews accompanying these stories in the Japanese media always paint a very pleasant picture of life outside the city. These stories of people who have escaped the crowding and long commutes associated with life in urban Japan have a nice escapist ring to those stuck in towns and cities. In truth there are very few of these people, far fewer than warranted by the attention the media gives to them. Unless one inherits a farm, there are few opportunities for livelihood outside of urban areas in Japan, and in spite of the vicarious pleasure people get from hearing the stories of u-turners, prejudice against country living is still a notable characteristic of Japanese culture.

SOME FEATURES OF MODERN JAPANESE CITIES

A visitor to Japan could not be blamed for puzzling over such a strong preference for city life. Except for just a few places such as parts of downtown Yokohama and some new towns like Tsukuba (a kind of upscale industrial park outside Tokyo), Japanese cities and towns don't usually strike non-Japanese as being very attractive. Although some of the recent architecture of the central parts of Japanese cities are exciting, there is rarely a sense of continuity in the Japanese urban landscape. Zoning has usually been avoided in Japan to support and encourage small businesses, resulting in what may be good for business but not for creating a pleasant visual environment. Because Japan is so land-poor, plots of land are sometimes unbelievably tiny; buildings of divergent sizes, styles, and ages are packed together on them in a visually dizzying mess.

For a nation with over 125 million people, as we have discussed, the geographic area of Japan is not very big. To make matters worse, the country is very mountainous, making the actual area available for urban development less than one-tenth the total landmass. On top of this, Japanese tax laws encourage people with a little extra space to keep plots of land as large food-producing gardens. Even though they may live only minutes from the centers of large cities and are in every sense city dwellers, they are officially classified as farmers and pay almost no real estate taxes on their entire adjoining property. This of course adds to the shortage of land for housing.

It is hardly surprising then to learn that urban Japan is a very crowded place with space a highly valued luxury. Living accommodations are compact; roads and highways are narrow even by the standards of the smaller European countries; park space is less available than in most other nations; in fact, almost everything that requires a place for it to exist is in short supply or at least downsized compared to its counterpart elsewhere. Garbage trucks are a perfect example of downsizing. From a distance, garbage trucks in Tokyo and other cities of Japan look exactly like the ones developed for use in American cities. They have the same hydraulic arms that extend the garbage bucket to the back of the truck and all the way in front over the cab and the same stuffer that compacts the load into the truck. On closer approach, however, a visitor from abroad suddenly realizes that they are in a sense scale models, about one-half the size of trucks in the United States. They have to be to squeeze through some of the tiny residential lanes in Japanese urban space.

Housing

Japanese share one cultural characteristic with Americans: the desire to live in a privately owned detached house is widespread and quite strong. For reasons pointed out above, this is less possible than in the United States. People in Japan often have to make a choice between two alternatives: to live in a house located far away from the business district of an urban area and endure a long, exhausting commute to work, or to live in one of the hundreds, or in some cases thousands, of little apartmentlike cells in a *danchi*, the condominium complexes that dot the urban landscape usually a little closer in than the single-home residential areas. The reason for the dilemma is that land prices are almost perfectly correlated to distance from the central parts of cities. The closer to the center, the more expensive; the further out, the more affordable. Danchi life often, but not always, offers escape from the grueling trip back and forth to work (two hours or more each way is quite common for those living outside urban areas), but it is not a very attractive compromise. A family of three or four people supported by an adequate income, but with no more than 500 or 600 square feet between them, roughly the area of a small one-bedroom apartment in the United States, is not the kind of life one would expect in a country with one of the highest per capita GNPs in the world. On the other hand, a two-hour train ride to work is not exactly luxurious living either.

Not all Japanese have to make a choice between these two less-than-ideal alternatives. Some lucky people inherit a house close to the urban core. Such property will probably stay in the family for the foreseeable future, because to sell it would be to turn over a very high percentage of the sale price in taxes, typically around 40 percent, but to keep it requires only a comparatively modest annual property tax. However, even these fortunate few must make some sacrifices. If people who manage to live in crowded neighborhoods close to the business district want to own and operate an automobile, municipal regulations require that they park it off the street overnight. In Tokyo, in fact, proof of a parking space is required by the city government before one can even buy a car. Only rarely is there room on the property for a private garage; typically they will have to rent space in a parking facility for several hundred dollars per month.

Another way some people who live in crowded urban Japan avoid at least the stress of commuting to work is by living at their work. Merchants in Europe and the United States normally close down their small business enterprises after a day's operation and travel back to a separate residence. In Japan, with property values comparatively higher on average than in Europe and the United States, small business owners find it is simply too expensive to maintain two properties, one for business and one for residence. The most common practice is to operate a business out of the ground floor of a small building, with the owner and his family using the second and other floors as residential areas. Until 150 years ago, cottage industry was the only type of business in Japan, and today merchants are still referred to as *honya-san*, "the book house family;" *nikuya-san*, "the butcher house family;" *denkiya-san*, "the electric utensils house family;" and so on.

URBAN INFRASTRUCTURE AND ORGANIZATION

When they talk about city life most Japanese do the same thing we do—they focus on the bothersome nature of urban environment. To Americans, for example, Japanese people often refer to their homes as "rabbit hutches." People tend to be more conscious of what is wrong with any social arrangement than with what works well. Crowded, yes; beautiful, not usually—but neither is urban Japan a place of teeming masses miserably unhappy and poorly served. A more balanced view reveals that Japanese towns and cities are in some ways models of civility with excellent facilities and a successful strategy in the face of difficult circumstances. Public transportation is one of those impressive aspects of modern urban Japan. Hundreds of miles of interurban train tracks crisscross the landscape of the largest cities; trains leaving heavily populated suburbs to carry passengers to their work in downtown areas arrive at stations every few minutes during commute hours. These trains are very crowded during rush hours, but the service is dependable, with train personnel as courteous and helpful as situations allow. Eight Japanese cities have subway systems; the network under the streets of Tokyo is second in total miles only to that in New York City and it is growing in size every 10 years, whereas the system in New York has not increased significantly in recent years. Many observers expect the Tokyo system to be the largest in the world in the near future.

The lack of urban zoning, although contributing to visual messiness as mentioned above, does have a positive side. For people who live in the built-up parts of towns and cities, shopping is much more convenient than the typical situation in the United States. Very few places in Japan are zoned only for residential use with merchants prohibited from running businesses from their property. As neighborhoods develop, consumer businesses sprout and develop along with them, so most people can shop for food or other necessities of daily life within only a short few-minute walk, instead of having to drive, park, and go through all the fuss required of most Americans.

Urban anonymity and indifference to shared communal interests has always been a drawback to city life everywhere. It is common for next-door neighbors not to know each other in modern urban residence areas all over the world, especially in large apartment complexes. The Japanese have some of this problem too; in fact, in some ways the Japanese are more indifferent to strangers in public than are Europeans and Americans. Japanese urban communities, on the other hand, try to work against that kind of disunity with all sorts of communal organizations, some of which work very well and have the effect of bringing a bit of village communalism to life in the faceless city. Many urban communities have neighborhood cleanup days, during which a member of each residence unit contributes a few hours to tidying up the area. It is common for older neighbors in Japanese cities and towns to form tour groups, traveling to hot-springs resorts and even taking trips to foreign countries together. Where one would expect the most facelessness of all, the large danchi complexes, there are usually various kinds of organized activities, including shared child care and different kinds of hobby groups.

So although it is not usually possible for the Japanese urban population to avoid conditions of crowdedness, the people bring considerable resourcefulness to the problems they have to face. Both authors have lived in urban Japan for a number of years at different times. Occasionally we yearned to get away from our cities, a feeling shared by city dwellers the world over. But even as Americans accustomed to much more space, we made successful adjustments, missing a few things from our former environments but enjoying some of the particular benefits Japanese cities offer.

THE KANTO REGION—TOKYO AND YOKOHAMA

It is difficult to understand urban Japan without taking a closer look into the character of some of the largest and most important Japanese metropolitan areas. The meaning of the two Chinese characters used in writing the word *Kanto* is "east of the gate," originally referring to the area to the east of an important checkpoint used to monitor movement of people back and forth between Edo and Kyoto by the Tokugawa regime in the Edo period (1600–1868). Today it is used to mean the huge metropolitan area around the capital of Japan, including the cities of Tokyo, Yokohama, and several hundred square miles of satellite cities and suburbs. It is the place where decisions are made that affect the economies of nations all across the globe. The Tokyo area is the nerve center of what is now and will remain for many years the most dynamic economy of Asia.

With nearly 20 million inhabitants, the Kanto region is the largest metropolitan area by far in Japan, and second in Asia only to Shanghai. The French, Russians, and Mexicans can easily understand the central place of Tokyo in Japanese life. In their countries, as well as in Japan, so much is both drawn to and emanates from a dominating capital city. Americans might have a harder time with this concept because American culture derives out of many regional urban areas, some of which play a dominant role in a particular industry: Detroit in the automotive industry, Pittsburgh in the steel industry, Southern California in the movie industry, and so forth. No one city in the United States is at the heart of all facets of national life. In Japan, Tokyo does indeed dominate virtually every aspect of that society; it is the political center, the nucleus of business and financial life, the entertainment center, the hub of national rail and air travel, the center of national and international communications, and the place where 5 of the top 10 universities are located.

Except for a very few corporations, such as the Toyota Motor Company centered in Nagoya, all large Japanese enterprises have their main offices in the Tokyo area even if they manufacture most of their products elsewhere. Many Japanese complain that the nation is far too centered around the capital and its surrounding area, causing everything—government, businesses, services of all kinds, and above all, people—to be squeezed into that one place of a few hundred square miles, smaller, as mentioned in Chapter 1, than the urban area around Los Angeles. In a nation without much land for urban space, the area around Tokyo is the most crowded of all. The Kanto region is the place where the most opportunities exist for high-paying jobs, higher education, and political influence. This creates an artificially high value of real estate and also contributes to more crowding than would be the case if these things were more spread out over the nation.

Although a lot of people who live in the Tokyo-Yokohama area would actually prefer to live in a smaller city and find life in the Kanto region a bit overwhelming, most Japanese are proud of their capital city. School children take group tours during both their tenure in junior high school and senior high school, and a common destination for school trips in the provinces is Tokyo. They visit the Imperial Palace; the National Diet building, which houses both houses of the Japanese legislature; Meiji Shrine, the large park dedicated to the first emperor of the modern period; and Tokyo Tower, modeled after, but slightly taller than, the Eiffel Tower in Paris. A large percentage of adult Americans, certainly more than half, have never visited New York City or Washington, DC. To meet an adult Japanese who has never been to Tokyo is a rare experience.

THE KANSAI REGION—OSAKA, KYOTO, AND KOBE

Some 300 miles to the southwest of the Kanto region is the second largest metropolitan area in Japan, the Kansai region, "west of the gate." In current usage, *Kansai* refers to the area around the city of Osaka and includes the cities of Kobe (where a calamitous earthquake did billions of dollars of damage and caused the deaths of more than 6,000 people in 1995) and Kyoto, the capital city of Japan for over 1,000 years until the middle of the last century. Japanese call this complex the Kansai region. With somewhere between six and seven million people, the area has only a third the population of the area around Tokyo, and today it is not the center of very much of national life. But the history of the Kansai region goes back much further than that of Tokyo, and many people who live there are convinced that their area, Kansai, and not Kanto, is the real heart of Japanese culture.

The Tokugawa shoguns, the regime that reigned over Japan from 1600 to 1868, in a real sense stole the center of Japanese life from Kansai and moved it to Kanto. True sons and daughters of Kansai have never quite forgiven this theft, and though most important institutions were eventually drawn to the new capital, in their hearts they consider Tokyo an upstart region full of displaced farmers. An interesting symbol of this pride is the way media personalities in Kansai, for example, people who read the news on local television, continue to speak Japanese with a distinctive rhythm and accent, whereas television news in the rest of the nation has succumbed to imitating the speech patterns of Tokyo.

Osaka itself had its origins as a commercial center and even now still has the reputation of a place where business interests take center stage. This is one of the reasons that among large cities of the developed world, it has a notoriously small amount of public park space. Osaka merchant families were the first to develop modern capitalism in Japan; some of the most famous names in Japanese business history—Mitsui, Sumitomo, Nomura, Matsushita—originate from Osaka; a few of them were famous even before the modern period in Japan began in 1868.

American military commanders were ordered not to bomb the city of Kyoto during the war with Japan, and so it escaped the destruction rained down on most of the other urban centers. It exists today as it has for centuries, an architectural record of Japanese history. There are over 500 temples of historical significance in Kyoto, some dating back to the ninth century. Those, together with some of the most famous gardens in the world, as well as the old Imperial Palace, draw more tourists than any other place in the country, both foreign and native. If one were limited to just a single place to see as a tourist in Japan, Kyoto would probably be the best choice.

SAPPORO

The northernmost and second largest island of the Japanese archipelago, Hokkaido, was the last area to be brought into the sociological and economic orbit of Japanese life. As late as 1910, less

Shinjuku, gateway to the western suburbs of Tokyo, on a Sunday afternoon. Vehicle traffic is rerouted so shoppers can use the entire area for strolling and shopping.

than 2 percent of the Japanese population lived there, and its capital, Sapporo, was little more than a military post near the middle of the island surrounded by a town of hardy pioneers. A Japanese Rip Van Winkle from that time could not believe what he would see a scant 90 years later. For decades it has been the fastest-growing urban area in Japan, recently passing Nagoya as the nation's third-largest city with a population of close to four million.

Besides Kyoto, which lies next to a large lake, Sapporo is the only other large Japanese city that is not a seaport; it is located about 50 miles inland from the nearest port of Otaru. Most of Sapporo's growth has taken place since the 1950s; thus as it grew it had a distinct advantage over older Japanese cities in being able to accommodate modern street planning and motorcars. We mentioned above that Japanese cities usually do not appear very attractive to outsiders. Sapporo comes closer than most to avoiding that characterization; in fact, some parts of the urban area are rather handsome. Streets in residential areas are laid out in straight lines and cross each other at right angles, a rarity in the rest of Japan (except for much of Hiroshima, which is also, in a sense, new). Street numbering in Sapporo is consecutive, as in most of the rest of the world, and does not follow the maddening chronological numbering system the Japanese traditionally have used. (It may be hard to believe, but the normal way of numbering properties in Japan is according to the date of their development within a relatively small area, so that number 5 may be next to number 18.) The downtown area, while certainly not on the level of a San Francisco or Seattle, has a certain functional attractiveness to it. One notable feature is the underground city, a shopping area one story under the surface of the central part of downtown that stretches for many blocks, a convenience for shoppers on cold Hokkaido winter days.

Sapporo's fantastically rapid development was the result of several factors. Wheat and dairy products began to catch on in Japan in the 1950s, and because Sapporo is too far north for successful rice production, the several thousand square miles of rich soil surrounding Sapporo was available and quickly became the source of two new massive industries—wheat products, especially wheat noodles, and a wide range of dairy products. A second source of growth is tourism; the area is second only to Kyoto as a destination for tourists. As Japan joined the ranks of affluent populations of the world, skiing became a popular recreation. With long winters and situated as it is close to mountains perfect as ski slopes, Sapporo rapidly grew into the winter sports and recreation capital of Japan. But it is not just a winter destination for Japanese travelers. Hokkaido has a climate unlike that of any other part of the nation. It is outside the range of rain clouds that cover Japan for most of the spring and early summer, which make a sunny day during those months a rare treat. It is also far enough north to escape the scorching heat and humidity of Japanese summers; thus Sapporo is an attractive tourist destination the year round.

CONCLUSION

In Japan, a preference for urban life is relatively high, certainly higher than for Americans. Unlike British and American historical experiences, rural life in Japan has not been associated with romantic images or with the residences of powerful elite. Most cities in Japan developed around castles during the fifteenth and sixteenth centuries, the centers of civilization and all political power.

In spite of the strong preference for city life, there are serious problems in Japanese urban life. Cities in Japan are among the most crowded on earth for several reasons, including a shortage of land suitable for urban development, tax laws that encourage people to keep land undeveloped, and the extreme concentration of government and big business in and around major cities. Housing costs in large cities are directly related to distance from city centers; for people of modest means, long commutes to work are common. Some people compromise by living in enormous apartment-like residential units, with individual units usually no more than the size of one-bedroom apartments in the United States.

There are positive aspects to urban life in Japan, including the country's famous low crime rate; almost all areas of urban life are safe at any hour of the day or night. The Japanese have tied their larger urban areas together with some of the most sophisticated public transit systems seen anywhere. Rail transit in all of its forms is probably more developed in Japan than in any other nation. There are no residential zoning laws in Japan, and although this can detract from appearance and quiet of residential areas, it also results in convenience for daily shopping because most consumer needs are just minutes away by foot.

Japanese life is more centered in a single capital city than in countries such as Germany or the United States, where industry, government, media, and education are more spread around. The Tokyo area, or the Kanto area as it is called in Japanese, has more than 20 million inhabitants and is the center of all important aspects of the nation. A few hundred miles to the southwest is the area called Kansai, including the cities of Osaka, Kobe, and the ancient capital of Kyoto. Natives of Kansai consider their region to be the cradle of Japanese civilization, with the Tokyo area a mere upstart instigated artificially by the Tokugawa shoguns a mere 400 years ago.

Finally we glanced briefly at Japan's newest and fastest-growing metropolis, the area around the city of Sapporo, the capital of the northern island of Hokkaido. More than any other city in Japan, Sapporo is truly of the twentieth century.

CHAPTER 11

Social Problems in Modern Japan

Just a few years ago there seemed to be a flood of books about Japan with titles such as *Japan as Number One* and *The Japanese Miracle*. Certainly there is much to be admired in Japan: the country has low rates of divorce, crime, unemployment, poverty, AIDS (0.3 per 100,000 population compared to the U.S. rate of 155.7), teenage pregnancy (only 1 percent of births are to teenage mothers compared to 20 percent for the United States); there are almost no guns, very little drug use (1 offender per 100,000 population compared to the U.S. rate of 346), and high rates of the positive things like literacy, high school completion, and life expectancy (Shapiro 1992). Americans visiting Japan for the first time are always amazed by these conditions because the contrasts to the United States are so striking.

So what can we possibly have to say about the subject of social problems that will cover a whole chapter in a little book on the Japanese society? For one thing, the perception of social problems in Japan can be instructive to Americans. While both authors were living in Japan, for example, we once saw a newspaper headline about the murder of a police officer in Tokyo. The article went on to say that Japan was getting as bad as the United States: "there have been over a dozen police killed in Tokyo . . . in the last 40 years." Another Japanese newspaper headline read, "Government Commission Says Japanese Schools Must Copy the United States." Knowing the high dropout rates, low test scores, frequency of school violence, and other negative aspects of American schools, we were quite interested in reading this article. As it turned out, the article was about low creativity and the lack of critical thinking among Japanese young people, certainly problems for a modern industrial giant.

Perhaps more important for our subject, there is, unfortunately for the Japanese, a downside to what Americans see as the low rate of social problems in Japan. For one thing, Japan is changing and some of these standard social problems are becoming more worrisome to the Japanese, even if the levels of these problems are much below those of the United States. In addition, many of the reasons for Japan's low rate of social problems would themselves be seen as social problems in the United States. Further, many conditions accepted and even valued by Japanese people would be seen as social problems by Americans. For example, in large part, crime is low because there are fewer freedoms and the police keep a close watch on all households in the nation; the divorce rate is low, in part, because women have few acceptable options to staying married.

In this chapter we first examine some of the traditional social problems such as poverty, crime, race and ethnic discrimination, suicide, and mental illness. And we will consider why these social problems are lower or different in Japan as compared to in the United States. In essence, following in the sociological tradition of Durkheim, we can learn a lot about a country by the kind of deviance and other social problems considered important by the people.

DEFINING SOCIAL PROBLEMS

Before proceeding we must note that defining **social problems** is no simple process. One country's social problems can be another's accepted or even valued state of affairs. What comes to be defined as a social problem depends on two important and interrelated factors: *values* and *influence*. As we have already seen, many cultural values differ between countries such as Japan and the United States, and these values set the stage for what we see as good or bad. Influence or power is important because what may be considered a social problem to some never come to be defined as such due to their lack of power. For example, sexual discrimination and sexual harassment in the workplace are only now becoming defined as significant social problems in Japan as women have become more organized and able to make the nation recognize these situations as problems.

POVERTY AND SOCIAL WELFARE

From what we have covered in our chapter on the Japanese economy, one might assume that poverty is not much of a social problem in Japan. With respect to the amount of poverty in Japan, the assumption is correct. During the early 1990s Japan was experiencing its highest levels of unemployment since recovery from World War II, at just over 3 percent. And although the level of unemployment is not always related to the level of poverty in a society (a high percentage of the poor are in fact employed in the United States, for example), the two are related in Japan. It is hard to compare poverty accurately across countries because all governments do not measure and define it in exactly the same way, as shown in Table 11–1, but the best estimates are that Japan has a poverty rate in the 1.5 to 2 percent range compared to 13 to 15 percent in the United States (Kerbo 1996: 467).

It is interesting to examine why poverty is so low in Japan. A comparison of most European countries, the United States, and Japan shows that the United States has the highest levels of poverty and by far the lowest per capita spending on social welfare programs to

TABLE 11–1

Percentage of Population Living in Poverty, Major Industrial Nations, 1984–1987

Country	All Persons	Children in Poverty
United States	13.3%	20.4%
Canada	7.0	9.3
Australia	6.7	9.0
United Kingdom	5.2	7.4
France	4.5	4.6
Netherlands	3.4	3.8
Germany	2.8	2.8
Sweden	4.3	1.6
Japan	2.0	—

Source: Adapted from Shapiro (1992), p. 74; Mishel and Bernstein (1993), p. 434; and Kerbo (1996), p. 248.

reduce poverty. Europe has low levels of poverty but high levels of government spending for unemployment benefits and social welfare programs. Japan, on the other hand, has low levels of poverty *and* low levels of welfare spending per capita (Mishel and Bernstein 1993; Kerbo 1996: 248, 488–89). In other words, the United States has high poverty and does little about it, European countries generally have high unemployment rates (now often over 10 percent) but low poverty because of government programs to reduce it, and Japan has low poverty without much government welfare spending (Verba et al. 1987). Japan has been able to keep poverty low simply because of high employment and average wages that are clearly sufficient to keep people out of poverty. Another factor, more in contrast to the United States than Europe, is Japan's strong family system. When a Japanese person is in financial trouble due to illness or joblessness, his or her family will usually provide plenty of help. Finally, as noted in earlier chapters, in Japan a good educational system is accessible to all and relatively few people experience racial or ethnic discrimination, both of which help reduce the number of people who might fall into poverty.

We are not suggesting that poverty does not exist in Japan, only that it is less of a social problem. Because there is so little government aid for the poor and unemployed in Japan, those who are poor without significant family contacts to help them are in serious trouble. There are pockets of poverty in big cities and even some hopelessness, such as the "day laborers" section of Osaka called Airin where there are about 20,000 low-income day laborers, of whom perhaps 300 to 1,000 are homeless (*Japan Times International Weekly*, November 8, 1992; November 13, 1995), and in the San'ya section of Tokyo (Fowler 1996). But the contrast to large American cities, where as many as 30,000 can be found homeless in each, must not be overlooked.

CRIME

Yes, compared to all other advanced industrial societies, especially the United States, the streets are safe in Japan. White-collar crime by corporations may be a different matter, and politicians are most likely more corrupt than in other industrialized countries (Kerbo and McKinstry 1995: Chap. 6). Comparing statistics for traditional street crimes (robbery, rape, and so forth) across nations is tricky because of differing methods and effectiveness of measures. But when it

TABLE 11–2

Comparative Crime Figures*

Country	Annual Murders per 100,000 Population	Percent of Population Victimized by a Crime
United States	9.4	28.8%
Canada	5.5	28.1
France	4.6	19.4
Germany (West)	4.2	21.9
England	2.0	19.4
Japan	1.2	9.3

* Figures are for various years in the late 1980s.

Source: Shapiro (1992), pp. 118, 120.

comes to comparing traditional crime rates between Japan and the United States, the statistics would have to be off many percentage points to reverse the above observation. In a typical year, the United States has from 5 to more than 100 times the amount of crime found in Japan (depending on the type of crime). Table 11–2 compares murder rates, which are rather easy to measure across nations, and the results of crime victimization survey, which are also generally reliable. Crime has gone up slightly in the last couple of decades in Japan, but there has been nothing like the increases experienced in the United States (Keizai Koho 1995; *Japan Times International Weekly*, October 21, 1996).

When we raise the issue of crime in Japan as contrasted to in the United States, the questions that come to mind concern not so much why it exists but why there is so little. The answers are complex and many; no one single factor is clearly the most important in keeping the level of crime low in Japan. But among the important reasons are the normally group-oriented Asian culture, which provides restraints on individual deviance; strong families; low inequality and poverty; and the nature of the Japanese criminal justice system.

We can consider the most complex answer first: the Japanese culture. Clearly this is not an exclusive reason for low crime in Japan because there have been higher levels at times in the nation's history. And because a culture is not very changeable, this explanation is not enough. Having said this, however, we must not exclude culture as one of the reasons. As described early in this book, there is a propensity for Japanese people to avoid conflict and obey the rules, which can help keep the crime rates low.

In regard to another of the cited reasons for low crime, we have already seen that Japan has one of the world's strongest family systems, with very few children lacking sufficient care. As all theories of the causes of street crime suggest, the way children are treated and cared for (or not cared for) affects the level of crime in a society. It is also clear that rates of poverty and, perhaps more important, the level of inequality in a society are factors (Blau and Blau 1982; Williams 1984; Muller 1985). Japan, as we have seen, has one of the lowest rates of income inequality and poverty; the United States has the highest. We can consider some other possible causes of low crime in more detail.

The Criminal Justice System

It seems likely that the nature of the Japanese criminal justice system is important in keeping crime low, but we cannot say exactly how much or even why. Let's consider, though, some of the important differences between the Japanese and U.S. criminal justice systems and the aspects of the former that many believe keep crime low.

The police force is most often cited. Japanese police are well trained and usually have college degrees; they are highly respected, certainly never feared, by the Japanese population. However, the Japanese police also have the ability to do many things not accepted in the United States (Ames 1981). For example, in every Japanese community, and in local neighborhoods in the large cities such as Tokyo and Osaka, there is a small police box called a *koban* always manned by at least one police officer. These officers keep close watch on the comings and goings of everyone in the neighborhood and are required by law to check homes regularly in order to keep records on who lives in the specific houses, their occupations, and other pertinent details about the people. *All people* living in Japan must register with the local government and police when they move into the area. Not knowing this, a foreigner living in Japan would likely be shocked to receive a knock on the door early one morning by a police officer in regular uniform, gun at his side, and clipboard in hand. It is, however, common practice.

What this means is that when a crime is committed in the neighborhood, the police usually have some ideas about who to talk to and find, or at least their good relations with the people of the community allow for many eyes watching to report things. A result is that the arrest rates per 100 offenses in Japan are about 95 percent for murder and 80 percent for robbery; they are about 70 and 25 percent, respectively, in the United States (Keizai Koho 1995; *Japan Times International Weekly*, October 21, 1996).

The treatment of suspects arrested for crimes in Japan also differs dramatically from that in the U.S. criminal justice system. Japanese police can hold a suspect for interrogation up to 23 days without interference by defense council for the accused. When a suspect is brought to trial, 99 percent are convicted by a panel of three judges (there are no jury trials in Japan), with over 80 percent convicted upon signed confessions during police interrogations (Ames 1981). As one might suspect, there have been many cases of people convicted of crimes they did not commit, with some in prison for decades before the fact was discovered. Groups both in and outside Japan, such as the United Nations and Amnesty International, have been increasingly critical of these aspects of the Japanese criminal justice system.

After a person is convicted of a crime, however, the United States and Japan differ in the other direction. Few convicted criminals in Japan are given prison time, with Japan having one of the lowest per capita prison populations in the world; the United States has the highest. In Japan it is assumed that the shame of conviction, along with little chance of getting a good job and the constant watch by the local police after release, is enough to deal with the problem. For those sent to prison, however, the treatment is tough; there is almost no freedom, with very rigid rules regulating all aspects of life behind bars, and almost no attempts at rehabilitation (*Japan Times*, March 31, 1996). There are executions in Japan, though fewer than in the United States and with a different philosophy: death sentences are reported in Japan, but there is no publicity when the execution is finally carried out.

Bōsōzoku: Youth Gangs

Although Japan is relatively free of most serious types of street crime, there is certainly no absence of many kinds of less serious deviance. An important example in recent years has been the disruptions and trouble caused by youth gangs. An image of L.A. street gangs and drive-by shootings, however, is not part of the Japanese scene; more typical is a rowdy street party and motorcycle races, with engines revved up as loud as possible at, say, 3 AM in the center of town. The chief activists in this type of deviance are motorcycle gangs called *bōsōzoku* (Sato 1991), made up of young people in their teens or early 20s who are clearly perceived as losers in the Japanese society. These are the young who have not tested well enough to get into the good high schools that prepare people for college or the good technical high schools that lead to well-paying working-class jobs. These young people are often in the vocational night schools clearly seen as dead ends (Rohlen 1983).

The Japanese society is a tough place for these young people, with no second or third chances in an educational system very different from that in the United States. Their bōsōzoku activities are a form of rebellion against this society that has shut them out of the legitimate opportunities to succeed. At the same time, however, bōsōzoku membership can be a means of illegitimate achievement, as many theories of youth gangs in the United States have suggested. A high percentage of the organized crime figures in Japan, the *yakuza*, are recruited from these youth gangs, a kind of alternative means of social mobility and opportunity for these failures in the Japanese educational system.

Bullying

One of the most publicized problems of recent years, and one that Japanese people seem always to be asking Western social scientists to share some possible wisdom about, is bullying. Quite simply, the problem is groups of school children, otherwise decent and obedient, ganging up on some poor boy or girl with physical, but more commonly mental, harassment, until the victim will no longer attend school, or in extreme cases, commits suicide. The Japanese newspapers of late seem full of cases of children who have committed suicide, leaving behind heart-wrenching suicide notes saying they can't take the bullying any longer. The Japanese Ministry of Education claims that bullying has gone up 2.6 times from 1993 to 1994, with

56,000 cases reported (*Japan Times International Weekly*, February 11, 1996), though very few have caused deaths.

There is, as we have already discussed in our second chapter, a reason to expect behavior such as bullying to be comparatively high in Japan. The flip side to a high degree of in-group unity and homogeneity in a society, as many sociologists have shown—from one of the old masters, Georg Simmel (1905/1955), to Lewis Coser (1956, 1967)—is less tolerance for diversity or people who are simply different.

A comparative perspective on the violence resulting from bullying in Japan is necessary, however. When the Japanese Ministry of Education stresses that "over six suicides in 15 months have been due to this," we must note the vastly greater problem of violence in American schools. Although the Japanese propensity is toward group conformity that can cause children who somehow stand out to be picked on by others, there are many more reasons for the excessive violence in American schools. But it is interesting that with much less youth violence than in the United States, Japanese parents have become more outraged. The United States has become a much more violent society, so much so that Americans have become accustomed to it, whereas the Japanese have not.

Organized Crime

At least as much as the notorious Mafia in the United States, and likely much more, Japan has a bigger-than-life image of the yakuza. Like the U.S. Mafia, the yakuza are well organized into separate families and are involved in many kinds of illegal activities, from drug trafficking to prostitution to extortion. They even seem to look like the Hollywood version of American gangsters, wearing dark suits and black ties and driving big American cars. The latter are very rare in Japan and thus called "gangster cars" when seen on Japanese streets. (The complete body tattooing that is common among the yakuza, though, does not fit the American Mafia image.)

There are, however, many significant differences, though some are primarily matters of degree. For one thing, the yakuza are much less violent. One of us living in Hiroshima in the late 1980s (a central area for one of the largest yakuza families) was close to a rather rare, but in other ways not untypical, event: a hit man, out to get a rival gang member, using an old handgun to do his business, missed completely, managing only to put a couple of holes in the bullet train as it came to a stop at the station. Movies about the yakuza made in Hollywood and shown in Japan can receive much laughter, such as *Black Rain* with Michael Douglas, depicting the yakuza as having as much fire power as the Japanese military. In all of 1995, for example, Japan had only 34 people killed with guns (about a normal two-week number for Los Angeles), and 20 of these were yakuza related.

The yakuza started as professional gamblers (*bakuto*) and racketeering organizations (*tekiya*) in feudal times. But they also were much like Robin Hood characters acting on the behalf of peasants. Following these traditions, today the yakuza continue to have some local welfare functions. Thus, although their activities have always been focused on the illegal, there has been a kind of code of honor, seeing themselves as something like the old samurai "lone rangers" going about helping the common people in some form of trouble (Kaplan and Dubro 1986).

The Japanese national police office reported about 3,305 groups of yakuza, with about 88,000 members in Japan (Shinnosuke 1992). Recently these groups have been moving into more complex forms of legal and illegal business activities, and they made considerable money in the overheated real estate market of the 1980s. Many of the scandals surrounding savings and loan banks going broke in the mid-1990s as a result of bad real estate loans and much of the political corruption in the late 1980s and early 1990s involved yakuza groups. And some of the corporate scandals, too, have involved yakuza figures putting pressure on and bribing corporate officials, though almost none of this has occurred with the highest levels of corporate power in Japan.

RACE AND ETHNIC DISCRIMINATION

Japan has never had to perform the difficult task faced by many other societies of somehow bringing together large numbers of people divided by race or important historical differences such as religion or ethnic identity to form a nation. Social class divides large groups in Japan, but there is much less divergence in language and manner of living than in other capitalist nations (Kerbo 1996: Chap. 14). There are minority populations in Japan, however, and although they are small in comparison with those in other places, their problems are sometimes compounded by the Japanese expectation that everyone who lives in Japan is, or should be, the same.

About 150 years ago, at the time Japan first began to open its doors to the outside world after more than two and a half centuries of isolation, many members of the samurai elite who were totally against allowing any outsiders to enter and reside in the nation. They argued that Japan was a sacred place created by Shinto gods and that the act of non-Japanese even setting foot on her soil was sacrilege. A few foreigners were actually killed by fanatics who believed this way, and although cooler and more practical heads prevailed, enabling foreigners to be eventually safe in Japan, it points to an extreme version of a feeling Japanese people have tended to hold for a long time—that Japan is a place for people of the Japanese race and that anyone else who is there is a sojourner, a visitor who cannot join or blend in with the native population.

In the modern world this feeling has been tempered considerably. Today there are tens of thousands of non-Asian people who consider Japan their home. However, Japan remains the most homogeneous of all industrialized nations, and that extreme degree of homogeneity, together with specific developments in the nation's history, has given the Japanese a highly developed consciousness of the boundary between themselves and the rest of the world. This helps us understand why Japan has not accepted its share of the world's refugees and political asylum seekers, for which the country has been criticized by groups such as Amnesty International. For example, 1990 was a typical year: Japan accepted only 2, whereas the United States accepted almost 100,000 (*Los Angeles Times*, March 18, 1993).

Koreans

Of the two largest ethnic groups in Japan, we considered the interesting case of Burakumin in the chapter on social stratification. The other significant minority population in Japan is smaller in number even than the Burakumin population, but the issues surrounding their status and position in Japanese society are much more widely known. These are the approximately one million Koreans of Japan, actually easier to label in English than Japanese because in Japanese it is customary to identify people of Korean descent with either the Republic of Korea (South Korea) or the People's Democratic Republic of Korea (North Korea). People identified with South Korea are called *Zainichi Kankokujin*, "South Koreans in Japan," and those identified with North Korea are called *Zainichi Chōsenjin*, "North Koreans in Japan." We'll simply call them *Koreans of Japan*. In some ways the label fits well; most Koreans of Japan are indeed Korean in that they are still citizens of either South or North Korea. They also tend to think of themselves as set apart from the Japanese around them, which is to say, they identify themselves as Koreans.

Whether they become Japanese citizens or not, today people who are known to be of Korean ancestry have long experienced prejudice and discrimination in Japan. In public most use the Japanese family name forced on them before the end of the war, and in college or at work Japanese who don't know them well are not aware that they are any different from any other Japanese. At important junctures in their lives, however—being considered for a secure job with a bright future or marrying into a Japanese family—their identity as Koreans of Japan comes to the surface, and many young Koreans of Japan confront a quiet but solid wall of rejection (De Vos and Wagatsuma 1966).

Decades of discrimination have produced an all-too-familiar pattern of reaction: Many Koreans suffer from low self-esteem; only a little over half of males finish high school, versus 97 percent for the nation as a whole; young men tend to drift into blue-collar jobs with little chance for middle-class attainment. A few have achieved great wealth; the Lotte chewing gum and candy company, the largest of its kind in the country, was founded by a Korean of Japan. But that is certainly not a typical case. Most Koreans with a penchant for business have been forced into areas often shunned by other Japanese, areas tinged with a questionable reputation such as money lending or the huge pachinko or pinball industry. That type of reaction to prejudice, of course, verifies deeply held stereotypes that place Koreans of Japan in a category beneath respectable middle-class Japanese society.

Problems faced by Koreans of Japan persist, but the climate for this group is unquestionably improving, as in the case of Burakumin. Korean organizations in Japan have been successful in bringing discrimination against the Koreans of Japan not only to the attention of the nation, but to some extent even to the world outside Japan. During the past few years, perhaps partly because issues surrounding Koreans of Japan were being discussed in international forums, a few court cases have been won by Koreans claiming discrimination against large corporations. Several Koreans, including noncitizens, have been allowed to become lawyers in a nation where entrance to that profession is carefully controlled by the government. And perhaps most significant of all, the youngest generation of adult Japanese are showing less willingness to continue the tradition of strong prejudice against people of Korean ancestry. Almost half of Koreans of Japan now marry native Japanese, up from less than 10 percent in the period following World War II. Fewer and fewer Japanese children find it necessary to conceal from their parents that they have a Korean friend. It is not likely that discrimination will disappear anytime soon, but already fewer young Koreans of Japan report harassment at school, which, if the trend continues, could signal a gradual end to the worst aspects of ethnic discrimination in Japan.

SEX AND THE SEX INDUSTRY

Considering the seriousness with which Japanese people seem to approach their work and the strength of the family system, Americans who have never been to Japan might assume Japanese people to be modest and prudish about sex. The assumption is quite wrong.

More like Europeans than Americans on this subject, as a whole Japanese people tend to be less uptight about matters of sex and sexual deviance. Homosexuality is not a big issue, and pornography is quite open, with sexually explicit magazines sold in vending machines on many street corners of Tokyo. It is not uncommon to see large ads showing women in only G-strings holding the featured can of beer. Perhaps more startling to foreigners are the sexually explicit comic books called *manga* that men read openly on the commuter trains and subways all over Japan. Some of these manga, in fact, have violent themes of rape, bondage, and brutality against women, which in the minds of most Japanese have now crossed the threshold of decency as evidenced by recent outcries in the Japanese mass media. All of these sexually explicit magazines, as well as movies, however, are covered by one basic censorship rule in Japan: no pubic hair can be shown. Beyond that, it is open. (And as you might expect, yes, there are employees of import houses who spend their days marking out the pubic hair in foreign magazines before they are sold.)

Probably most interesting are the "love hotels"; they are seen by the hundreds if not thousands all over Tokyo, and every city of any size has at least a few. Love hotels are simply hotels where couples pay for a room by the hour, with many sexually oriented devices and features supplied in the rooms (Bornoff 1991: 17). These places are all quite openly advertised as love hotels usually with purple lights outside. They have names such as "Love Haven" and special entrances so that customers can quickly enter and even hide their cars behind curtained driveways. Other countries, of course, have such love hotels, but in no other country we have seen are they so organized and openly displayed as love hotels and in such great numbers. (Thailand, for example, noted for its sex industry, is actually more modest about sex in some ways, and its love hotels are much more difficult to identify from a distance.) One reason for the demand for such numbers of love hotels in Japan, however, is rather understandable given crowded housing conditions, where few young people have cars or even apartments away from their parents before getting married in their late 20s or even early 30s.

Prostitution in Japan is illegal, but is also quite open. Virtually all cities have their brothel sections. Ads for house calls or hotel calls by these ladies are typically plastered all over phone booths and mailboxes, as well as handed out on busy street corners, though to some Japanese it has recently gotten out of hand (*Japan Times International Weekly*, September 30, 1996).

We have dwelled on the extent of sexual openness in Japan to make an additional point: The American assumption tends to be that sex openly displayed as it is in Japan will lead to extensive sexual deviance of the worst kind. In other words, increases in rape, teenage sexual activity and pregnancy, and so forth would result from loose controls on the open showing of sex in the society. However, much social science research shows, and the case of Japan makes clear, that the above assumptions are not accurate.

Crime statistics indicating that rape is relatively low in Japan have already been discussed. What is even more remarkable, however, is that for the most part the openness toward sex in Japan has not led to extensive sexual promiscuity among Japanese teenagers. It is impossible for young girls and boys to escape viewing such explicit sexual activity, and some of it can even be seen on the regular television channels on weekday afternoons. But for many years, studies have shown Japanese teenagers to have little involvement with sexual activity. For example, one study in the early 1980s indicated only 17 percent of senior high school girls and 25 percent of boys have had sexual intercourse (Rohlen 1983: 290). Another Ministry of Education national survey indicated that only 20 percent of somewhat younger teenagers had even kissed someone of the opposite sex.

There has been a long history of casual views toward sex and nudity in Japan. It was only with increasing Western contact and influence about 100 years ago that Japan became uncomfortable with such practices as same-sex public baths. Prostitution has been quite accepted through most of Japanese history, to the point that a couple of hundred years ago, much like theater and movie reviews in newspapers today, one could find such reviews of individual prostitutes and brothels (Buruma 1984: 76).

Japan, however, is changing. And although rape and other sexually related violent attacks remain relatively rare, other kinds of sexual deviance and crime seem to be increasing. One form that has become widespread and involves men is called *chikan*. Chikan are men who grab and fondle women on crowded trains. One survey found 80 percent of high school girls have been victims, but only 2 percent of these cases were reported to police. What is so striking to outsiders and Japanese as well is how this activity is so organized by the chikan. There are videos on how to do it and a popular magazine aimed at chikan.

Despite all we have said above, there is evidence that some young people are also changing, becoming more sexually active and involved in what most Japanese define as deviant types of activities. Throughout history, it seems, most societies have had their generational conflicts, with older adults saying the young no longer are as hardworking and moral. Such complaints have been heard for at least a couple of decades in Japan, but only now is there significant evidence to justify these beliefs by adults. With respect to our current subject, national surveys indicate that young Japanese women in their 20s, for example, are becoming more sexually active and delaying marriage as long as possible (*Japan Times International Weekly*, July 13, 1992). And during 1996, Japanese newspapers were filled with reports about telephone sex clubs. There is estimated to be 2,200 of these clubs in Japan, which operate by charging men about $20 to sit in a booth waiting for calls from teenage girls in response to the widespread ads.

Only a small percentage of Japanese girls have gone further than just call once and talk to the men for a few minutes, but girls who agree to have sex with these men usually get about $1,000 (*Los Angeles Times*, September 30, 1996).

SUICIDE

As most people are aware, suicide has a long tradition in Japanese society. Suicide was an honorable, even required, way of accepting defeat or failure, or to take oneself out of a situation to benefit the larger group. In a classic tale, "Forty-Seven Rōnin," leaderless samurai avenge the death of their feudal lord, and to maintain their honor after the forbidden act of revenge, they commit mass suicide. In real life, after defeat in battle, the samurai defending the feudal domain, their retainers, and even close relatives were required to atone for their shame by committing suicide. Even after the death of an emperor, many of his closest aides and sometimes dedicated followers would commit mass suicide. And of course, more recently, there were the famous kamikaze fighter pilots of World War II who flew planes loaded with TNT into American warships in their last efforts to win the war. As these examples show, this form of suicide is the essence of what the sociological master Émile Durkheim called **altruistic suicide** in his famous work *Suicide* published in 1899. Durkheim did not mention the Japanese tradition in this work, but he clearly should have as one of the best examples.

There remain some elements of this tradition of ritual suicide in Japanese society today—but only some. During 1989, for example, the manager of one of the most winning professional baseball teams in Japan committed suicide after a losing season. More recently, the director of a nuclear power plant committed suicide when it was found that his company covered up a leak of radioactive steam, as did the public school official in one large district who was in charge of school lunches after a food-poisoning outbreak made thousands ill in the summer of 1996. There have been recent cases of trusted aides committing suicide to protect their bosses during political scandals. But such extreme measures are now rare. More common is the practice of resignation to take responsibility for an agency's mistake or failure. Corporate scandals often lead to the resignation of the top executive who had no real responsibility for the scandal, as did the CEO of Japan

Airlines after a crash killed over 500 people in 1985; government officials may resign to apologize and take public responsibility for an accident or mistake, as did the head of Japan's Self Defense Force (Japanese military) when a submarine struck a fishing boat and killed several fishermen in 1988. It can be rather tough at the top in Japan, though luckily for corporate executives and government ministers actual suicide is no longer seen as appropriate.

An examination of comparative suicide rates today, as shown in Table 11–3, shows that Japan has only about an average number of suicides per 100,000 population. But a look within certain categories of the population will reveal some surprises. As many Americans might think after learning of the great pressures placed on Japanese children to get into a good university during "examination hell," and as the

TABLE 11–3

Comparative Suicide Rates, Early 1990s

Country	Rate (per 100,000 population)
Finland	27.6
Austria	21.3
France	20.3
Belgium	19.3
China	17.6
Japan	**16.6**
Germany	15.6
Sweden	15.6
Norway	14.4
Canada	13.0
United States	**12.2**
Australia	11.1
Singapore	10.6
Netherlands	10.5
Hong Kong	10.3
South Korea	9.4
England	8.0
Italy	7.8
Spain	7.5

Source: *UN Demographic Year Book* (New York: United Nations, 1994).

Japanese themselves assume, Japanese teenagers should have a very high rate of suicide. Indeed, every year after these exam results are announced, there are prominent news stories about a couple of teenagers throwing themselves in front of a train because they failed the exam. But though the Japanese rate of teenage suicide was among the highest in the 1950s, it has gone down considerably since and is relatively low today (Rohlen 1983: 329). And when we actually look at the figures, the U.S. teenage suicide rate is higher than in Japan. As Durkheim knew, if not in exact details, there are different causes of suicide, including both pressure and neglect.

Before leaving this subject, we can follow this cultural theme in Japanese history to make a point about other kinds of destructive behavior. It is interesting that while the suicide rate for the total population is greater in Japan than in the United States and vice versa for the murder rate, the sums of the two rates for each country are rather close. This is to say that in both countries people have about equal chances of dying at the hand of someone: the major difference is that in Japan you are more likely to do it yourself, whereas in the United States someone else is more likely to kill you. At least some of the difference comes from important cultural contrasts we have seen early in this book. In Japan, blame and frustration are less likely to be projected outward to others in the group than inward to the self. In recent years the United States has been called a "nation of victims": whatever is wrong is someone else's fault. Thus, when Japanese become frustrated or angry, they more often turn on themselves. Americans, on the other hand, turn their aggression outward and at times attack other people.

MENTAL ILLNESS

Of all the social problems, mental illness is probably the one most difficult to compare across cultures. Definitions of mental illness differ; what people think can and cannot be treated as mental illness differ; and the reactions to the existence of mental illness make some societies hide the problem, making any international comparisons about it difficult.

Although slowly changing, in Japan mental illness has been considered shameful and in the past hidden. The same has been the case with severe physical disabilities. One simple reason has been that mental illness or birth defects in the family make it difficult to find marriage partners. Family members of the prospective bride and groom may search for these hidden problems, sometimes through special private detective agencies, before they allow a marriage to proceed.

Only recently in Japan could you find mentally ill or severely disabled people out in public, though not employed in low-skilled jobs in restaurants or hotels as recently done in the United States. The Nobel Prize–winning author Kenzaburo Oe and his wife treated their autistic son, Hiari Oe, untypically, giving him music lessons when his amazing talents as a classical music composer were finally recognized.

Though we can not give much weight to official statistics about the rates of mental illness in Japan, how it is viewed and treated by psychologists, psychiatrists, and social workers is very instructive. Following our comparisons between the individualistic United States and the more group-oriented Japan earlier in this book, we can understand that psychological therapy techniques might differ in the two societies. With most mental illnesses in the United States, the goal of the therapist is to help the patient attain more self-reliance, self-autonomy, and even independence. Also, in the United States there is more concern among therapists that the group may be oppressive and dysfunctional for the person being treated. In Japan, on the other hand, the therapy is more likely oriented toward getting the person to fit in with the group, to accept one's place, and to develop and recognize a dependent relationship to another person similar to that of a child toward its mother (Doi 1981, 1986).

CONCLUSION

In this chapter we have considered how social problems are defined and examined several types of social problems in Japan today.

In general, Japanese do well by their poor, their sick, their children, and other people who cannot help themselves. But what is more unique about Japanese among the modern industrial societies is they do this with very little help from government agencies, with the exception of their very large and generous national health care system open to all citizens. The strong group orientation leads to taking care of "their own," meaning first other family members but also others who are considered part of whatever closely knit in-group, including employees of corporations. As we have seen, people are under great pressure to work hard in Japanese companies, but if they cannot for some reason, they are seldom fired. As we have noted, it is rather remarkable that with over five years of bad economic times in Japan from the early 1990s, the country's unemployment rate is still only in the 3 percent range. The reason is that Japanese corporations almost always hang on to their employees somehow, even if it means reduced profits, or find them other jobs with related corporations. Thus, there is much less need for government welfare programs in Japan.

CHAPTER 12

Social Change and Japan in the Twenty-First Century

A Conclusion

At the end of the twentieth century, many Japanese feel they are entering a time of crisis that must lead eventually to major changes. The Japanese economy seems no longer able to expand and challenge the world as during the decades before; the Japanese government seems to move from one scandal to another with no real reform taking hold. The political and economic system put together after World War II that helped Japan emerge from the ashes, and even create what was generally called the "Japanese miracle," no longer seems to be the political-economic system needed to keep Japan moving ahead as a competitive nation in the twenty-first century. As indicated in Chapter 6 on the power elite in Japan, many of the political and economic reforms that most Japanese people feel are needed have been blocked by these men of power who do not want change that will cut into their authority and privileges.

The change, however, involves more than a crisis in the political-economic system. Several other trends indicate that trouble is on the way: Japan will soon have the highest percentage of people over 65 than any other nation; more than in previous times, Japanese people are feeling overstressed and overworked from the demands of a highly competitive society; and more and more Japanese youth seem to be rejecting the old values of discipline and hard work.

In this final chapter we will look at some of these troubling trends in the Japanese society that will have a large impact on the future of Japan in the twenty-first century.

JAPAN'S AGING POPULATION

Ask average Americans about the population characteristics of Japan and perhaps 90 percent will say the country is overcrowded with people and growing as fast as, say, Pakistan. In fact, the general image of Asia in the eyes of North Americans and Europeans is one of too many people and a rapidly growing population. As we have noted many times, however, there is great variation among Asian countries, with some such as Thailand that have conquered their problems of rapid population growth to such an extent that they are worried about population decline. As for Japan, some urban areas are crowded, but many parts of rural Japan have actually become depopulated to such an extent that there are not enough people left to operate the rural economy effectively.

The Japanese birthrate is dropping, coming close to zero population growth. Most immediately, the concern is that Japan will soon have an even larger labor shortage. With the economic recession of the early 1990s, Japan had a small unemployment rate, but everyone knows this is only temporary. Major Japanese corporations have continued exporting much of their production overseas, particularly to other Asian countries, in part because of the labor shortage, in part because of the high value of the Japanese yen. Now many big Japanese manufacturing firms produce most of their products overseas, and a few even have no production in Japan any longer. Still, much work needs to be done back in Japan, and too few workers means a less competitive economy.

Some of the other advanced industrial societies in Europe, such as Germany, are also facing prospects of population decline due to such a low birthrate. The sharp decline in the Japanese birthrate, however, is a bit more complex and unclear. Many groups, especially those representing women in Japan, claim that the drop is due to the continuing difficult living conditions in Japan: houses are too small, commutes to work are too long, and basic necessities are more expensive than ever (*Los Angeles Times,* June 8, 1992; January 6, 1992). And with Japanese men working longer hours than in other countries, and

162   Chapter 12

thus less often at home, Japanese women have even more of the job of raising children and taking care of household duties than women in other countries. In addition, of course, there is the universal reason for declining births in advanced societies: women are seeking more freedom, thus delaying marriage and delaying having children or choosing to not have children at all (*Japan Times International Weekly*, July 13, 1992).

In about 25 years, 25 percent of Japan's population will be 65 years old or more, the highest percentage for any country in history. Currently Japan is rather close to the other advanced industrial nations with 12 to 13 percent of its population 65 years or older. But while this percentage is holding steady in other countries, it is changing rapidly in Japan. Somewhat like in the United States, there was a baby boom in Japan after World War II. In short, with the war over, more people could settle down to start families. From 2010 to 2025 these baby boomers will hit retirement age, bringing up the percentage of population 65 and over. In addition, however, Japanese people are living longer than any other people in the world, and the birthrate is now much below that of the United States. Currently Japanese women have the highest life expectancy at over 80 years, with Japanese men also the highest in the world at over 75 years. The United States and European countries will not change much from their current 12 to 15 percent of the population 65 and over because of less declines in birthrates, somewhat lower life expectancies, and sometimes more immigration.

These three factors add up to significant trouble in coming years for Japan. Most important, the problem is related to costs of health care. As one might think, elderly people need medical care more often on average; in fact, most nations spend the majority of their health care on the elderly. Japan, like every other advanced industrial country (except the United States), has a national health care system that pays the medical bills for all citizens through tax money. With 25 percent of the population elderly, that health care budget will skyrocket, and so will the taxes needed to pay for it.

There is another problem almost equally serious: Japan has one of the least developed old-age pension systems of advanced industrial nations, either through a government program such as Social Security in the United States, or private corporate pension/retirement funds. This is a primary reason that Japan has more people over 65 who are employed than any other industrial nation. The famous lifetime employment in Japan was always misleading. What happens is that employees of major corporations are forced to retire at 55 years old or so; they then must go to work at lower pay in a smaller affiliate company. But with the population growing ever older, these people are living way beyond 65 years and cannot continue to be employed. With this situation Japan will have to greatly expand its Social Security–type system to pay for the care of the elderly. Again, this will be very expensive. At present, Japan is like other industrial countries with about two or three workers to every retired person. This means that two or three working people are paying taxes or are having pension funds deducted to care for one retired person. It is easy to see the problem when the ratio of workers paying in and retirees taking out reaches one to one.

In the past, of course, and continuing in the present, the Japanese family is among the strongest in the world. Elderly people tend to live with their adult children. But this is becoming less so in Japan (though still much more than in the United States) with changing preferences, work mobility, and simply more older people to handle. Japanese welfare agencies are becoming quite innovative in attempting to deal with the problem, as well as helping adults cope with care for their elderly parents. Day care centers for the elderly, for example, are becoming more available in Japan. These are often very well equipped with game rooms and devices for the disabled, such as the remarkable machines that help raise and lower the elderly into the *ofuro*, the all-important hot bath that Japanese enjoy every day. But again, all of this costs money, and with 25 percent of the population elderly, the burden on the younger and employed will be great.

JAPAN'S STRESSED-OUT LABOR FORCE

Japan has a problem seldom heard of in the United States: *karōshi*, or death by overwork—most often simply death from exhaustion after too many hours of work over too many days. Japanese people work longer hours than people in any other advanced industrial nation. The average hours worked per year range from over 2,000 for Japanese people to about 1,600 for Germans, with Americans moving closer to the Japanese average in recent years. The problem of overwork in general is considered serious enough that the Japanese government has mounted an ad campaign in recent years telling people to stop working so many hours. There have been posters in trains asking everyone to please take all of their vacation time. Also, to set an example for the country, government offices are starting to close on Saturdays, and some corporations are actually requiring their office employees to stop work at least one day a week by 6 PM, in some cases cutting off electricity to the building to force them out. According to official statistics released by the government, the average rate of hours worked by the Japanese per year has actually gone below 2,000 hours in recent years (in other words, a full six-day workweek), but few people believe it. The pressure of the group on the job to work remains strong, and to make the company seem to fall in line with national demands to reduce working hours, many in management falsify the figures at the office level (*Japan Times International*, June 9, 1996).

Although karōshi is no doubt significant, with extreme estimates as high as 10,000 deaths a year, it is not the only problem associated with overwork (*Los Angeles Times*, January 14, 1992). With fathers going to work at sunup or before, and getting home at 11 or 12 at night, most children are being raised with very little fatherly contact. Most Japanese social scientists expect that such fatherly neglect must be taking its toll on children, especially young boys who are often lacking a strong role model. A recent survey of 3,000 children in Germany, Japan, and the United States, for example, found that Japanese children had the lowest level of respect for their fathers, much lower than in the United States (*Los Angeles Times*, July 6, 1993).

There is also the problem of expanding the domestic economy: Japan cannot forever keep its economy going by focusing on exporting goods to other countries like the United States. The country must increase domestic consumption, which requires giving employees more time off from work to stimulate it sufficiently. Thus, for various reasons overwork and its many consequences present major problems in Japan.

THE "ME GENERATION"

Although perhaps not of the order that older Japanese will feel comfortable with, solutions to the problems associated with overwork may be on the horizon. According to older Japanese, their young people are becoming more self-centered, less willing to sacrifice for the group (especially the work group), and much more concerned with leisure activities. Japanese teenagers, they say, show less respect for parents and teachers and are less likely to follow the value orientations of the older generation. In other words, the old methods of inducing conformity so successful with earlier generations of Japanese, as outlined early in this book, seem to be weakening.

Opinion polls consistently back up these statements, as do observations obtained by simply walking around Japan today. A few Japanese young people can be seen with colored hair (forbidden by most schools below the college level in the past), punk rock clothing styles, and other signs of youth rebellion against the values of their parents. Some Japanese, in fact, have begun calling this "the American disease." In the West, especially in America, young people have most always had a degree of independence and at least mildly rebelled against the values of their parents. In fact, in contrast to Japan, growing up in America has been a process of becoming independent from parents (White 1987). With the affluence of modern Japan, and perhaps because of more media influence from the Western industrialized nations, especially the United States, values of young Japanese are changing.

Other Japanese worry about whether the younger generation have any values at all. Japanese people were not only shocked that the religious cult, Aum Shinrikyō, tried to kill many Japanese in a gas attack in the Tokyo subway system a few years ago, as related in Chapter 8; they were also shocked that so many of Japan's best and brightest youth (such as top graduates from Tokyo University) had been attracted to the cult. We have noted that there are some 1,500 small religious cults operating just at the foot of the famous Mt. Fuji alone. The mid-1990s have brought a flood of news commentaries about the lost and alienated Japanese young people. A general theme is that the older generations were taught to value hard work as a means to material success. Japanese young people have material success; and other values, it is said, have not been forthcoming to give young people purpose and meaning in life.

Although the rebellion of the Japanese "me generation" may expand, from the American perspective, it remains on a relatively small scale. Drugs and sexual experimentation can be found in some of the disco areas of Tokyo. The fad for a couple of years in the early

1990s was clubs where frustrated young office ladies would take over the stage and strip. And we have mentioned the telephone sex clubs in the previous chapter. Still, this continues to involve only a very small percentage of Japanese young people. For example, most of the teenagers in black leather, long hair, and punk clothing seen dancing around Tokyo's large Yoyogi Park every Sunday afternoon in the thousands will change their clothing before going home to do their homework that night.

Whether or not outsiders agree with older Japanese that a problem actually exists (rather than a change to a more free and relaxed society), the presence of this me generation must be recognized as an agent of potential change in some of the basic characteristics of the Japanese society.

CONCLUSION

In a sense it can be said that Japan is reaching maturity. The nation began its process of industrialization only about 100 years ago, and much of it was delayed or reversed by World War II. The 1980s was the first time a large majority of Japanese ever experienced what anyone could call affluence. Affluence, it is often said, is one of the biggest stimulants for change: People live longer, there is a decline in the birthrate as there are more options in life and children become more expensive, and people are less motivated to work hard when they are well off and do not have to worry about living in the streets and facing starvation as did Japan's population in the 1940s and early 1950s. How much Japan will fall to the "American disease" is an interesting question for sociologists in coming years. As we have noted in the early chapters of this book, Japan was the first Asian nation to industrialize. The debate at the time concerned the ways in which Japan could do it and whether the country would become more Westernized in the process. Now the debate can turn to how the first Asian nation to achieve extensive prosperity for the masses will deal with the many problems, the "diseases," that rich nations face.

NOTES

1. It is this value orientation of "radical individualism" that is increasingly cited as partially responsible for many of our social problems—from the highest divorce rate and rate of single parent families among industrial nations, to the high crime rates and low educational success compared to other nations. See Bellah (1985) and Etzioni (1984).

2. For more detailed explanation of this type of historical and comparative research and the effects of the material environment, see Gouldner and Peterson (1962); Heise, Lenski, and Wardwell (1976); Lenski (1966, 1978); and Lenski and Nolan (1986).

3. For example, in Soseki's novel *Sore Kara* (And Then. . .) the main character defies accepted tradition and morality in his personal life; in *The Miner* the main character rejects his rigid middle-class world and escapes to the dirty, dangerous, but for him, a world of freedom, underground in the mines; in *Kōjin* (The Wayfarer) the main character struggles against conformity and produces the famous line, "To die, to go mad, or to enter religion—these are the only three courses left open to me"; in *Mon* (The Gate) the main character defies the authority of his parents to marry for love and is rejected by friends and family.

   The main point is that the theme of rebellion against society, parents, and others can be found throughout Japanese literature. Because the pressure on Japanese people to conform is great, the characters of Soseki's novels and those of others strike a desired emotion to rebel; but alas, the rebel usually gets it in the end, which also expresses an inner dread of Japanese people.

4. For examples of this from Japanese history, see Bowen (1980), Hane (1982, 1988), Apter and Sawa (1984), Mouer and Sugimoto (1986), and Pharr (1990).

5. See for example the classic works of Simmel (1905/1955), and the more recent works of Coser (1956, 1967), Sherif (1966), Kanter (1972), and Collins (1975).

6. There are recent indications of the reduction of lifetime employment in Japan even among the 30 percent of the labor force employed in the big core corporations. Due to the Japanese economic recession of the 1990s and increased competition with the United States, corporations are said to be firing or laying off some people. Extensive data indicating the magnitude of this change do not yet exist, however. There are national surveys of the general population that show less loyalty to a single employer and more willingness to change jobs. In 1987, for example, 42 percent of Japanese said they would be willing to leave a frustrating job to find a better one, whereas in 1995 over 63 pecent said they would do so (*International Herald Tribune*, June 13, 1996: 13). But it is interesting that in 1992, still only 44 percent said they would be willing to leave such a job, indicating real attitude changes only between 1992 and 1995. Thus, one wonders if

this is a real attitude change or just a short-term change of opinion due to the extent of the Japanese economic depression.

7. According to official Japanese government figures, since 1993 the average Japanese employee actually put in fewer hours per year than the average American. Officially, the hours worked per year for the average Japanese employee was 1,966 in 1993, compared to 1,976 in the United States. The hours worked by the average Japanese employee is no doubt going down. Most companies now have instituted a no-overtime day once a week (*no zangyo*), but this is usually not followed. A primary reason that the official Japanese government figures on hours worked are inaccurate is that they come from company reports, not directly from employees. Perhaps more important, however, is that most employees in Japan do not report all of their overtime. Some reasons for not reporting are that employees don't want to make the company look bad by not complying with government demands to reduce hours worked, but also employees often don't like to admit it takes them so long to do a certain job (*Japan Times*, June 9, 1996: 16).

8. There have been numerous studies of income inequality between workers and corporate executives in Japan, the United States, and other leading industrial nations such as Germany. Although the figures differ somewhat because of the number of industries included and time periods, all of the studies agree that the pay gap is much lower in Japan than in the United States, with Germany quite close to Japan in the worker-to-chief-executive pay gap. See, for example, Abegglen and Stalk (1985: 192), *The Wall Street Journal* (April 18, 1984), *The Wall Street Journal Europe* (October 9–10, 1992), and the *Los Angeles Times* (March 2, 1993).

9. Various studies have indicated that the status dimension of social stratification can be dominant only in societies with a very high degree of value consensus, such as religious monasteries or small collective communities (Rosenfeld 1951; Spiro 1970; Della Fave and Hillery 1980; Kerbo 1996: 127, 465). In other words, there must be extensive agreement on values if people are to concur as to who deserves status or honor rewards, and such agreement usually comes only in a small, homogeneous society.

REFERENCES

Abegglen, James C.; and George Stalk, Jr. *Kaisha: The Japanese Corporation*. New York: Basic Books, 1985.

Alletzhauser, Albert J. *The House of Nomura*. New York: Little Brown, 1990.

Ames, Walter L. *Police and Community in Japan*. Berkeley: University of California Press, 1981.

Apter, David E.; and Nagayo Sawa. *Against the State: Politics and Social Protest in Japan*. Cambridge, MA: Harvard University Press, 1984.

Atsuta, Masanori. *Shinzaikai Jinretsuden* (Biography of the new financial world lineup). Tokyo: Yomiuri Shimbunsha, 1992.

Beck, E.M.; Patrick Horan; and Charles Tolbert. "Social Stratification in Industrial Society: Further Evidence for a Structural Alternative." *American Sociological Review* 45 (1980), pp. 712–19.

Befu, Harumi. *Japan: An Anthropological Introduction*. New York: Chandler Publishing Co., 1981.

Bellah, Robert. *Tokugawa Religion: The Cultural Roots of Modern Japan*. New York: Free Press, 1985.

Benedict, Ruth. *The Chrysanthemum and the Sword: Patterns of Japanese Culture*. New York: Houghton Mifflin, 1947.

Blau, Judith; and Peter Blau. "The Cost of Inequality: Metropolitan Structure and Violent Crime." *American Sociological Review* 47 (1982), pp. 114–29.

Bornoff, Nicholas. *Pink Samurai: Love, Marriage and Sex in Contempory Japan*. New York: Simon and Schuster/ Pocket Books, 1991.

Bowen, Roger W. *Rebellion and Democracy in Meiji Japan*. Berkeley: University of California Press, 1980.

Brinton, Mary C. "Gender Stratification in Contemporary Urban Japan." *American Sociological Review* 54 (1989), pp. 549–64.

—————— . *Women and the Economic Miracle: Gender and Work in Postwar Japan*. Berkeley: University of California Press, 1991.

Buckley, Sandra; and Vera Mackie. "Women in the New Japanese State." In *Democracy in Contemporary Japan*, ed. Gavan McCormack and Yoshio Sugimoto, pp. 173–85. New York: M.E. Sharpe, 1986.

Buruma, Ian. *Behind the Mask*. New York: Meridian, 1984.

Clark, Rodney. *The Japanese Economy*. Tokyo: Tuttle, 1979.

Collins, Randall. *Conflict Sociology*. New York: Academic Press, 1975.

Cook, Alice H.; and Hiroko Hayashi. *Working Women in Japan: Discrimination, Resistance, and Reform*. Ithaca, NY: Cornell University Press, 1980.

Coser, Lewis. *The Function of Social Conflict*. New York: Free Press, 1956.

————. *Continuities in the Study of Social Conflict*. New York: Free Press, 1967.

Curtis, Gerald L. *Election Campaigning Japanese Style*. New York: Columbia University Press, 1971.

————. *The Japanese Way of Politics*. New York: Columbia University Press, 1988.

Della Fave, L. Richard; and George Hillery. "Status Inequality in a Religious Community: The Case of a Trappist Monastery." *Social Forces* 59 (1980), pp. 62–84.

De Vos, George; and Hiroshi Wagatsuma. *Japan's Invisible Race: Caste in Culture and Personality*. Berkeley: University of California Press, 1966.

Dietrich, William S. *In the Shadow of the Rising Sun: The Political Roots of American Economic Decline*. University Park, PA: Pennsylvania State University Press, 1991.

Doi, Takeo. *The Anatomy of Dependence*. Tokyo: Kodansha, 1981.

————. *The Anatomy of Self: The Individual versus Society*. Tokyo: Kodansha, 1986.

Domhoff, G. William. *The Powers That Be*. New York: Vintage Press, 1979.

————. *Who Rules America Now?: A View for the 80s*. Englewood Cliffs, NJ: Prentice Hall, 1983.

Dore, Ronald. *Taking Japan Seriously*. Stanford: Stanford University Press, 1987.

Durkheim, Émile. *Suicide*. New York: Free Press, 1951.

————. *Elementary Forms of the Religious Life*. New York: Free Press, 1954.

Etzioni, Amitai. *An Immodest Agenda for Rebuilding America before the 21st Century*. New York: McGraw-Hill, 1984.

Fallows, James. *Looking at the Sun: The Rise of the New East Asian Economic and Political System*. New York: Pantheon, 1994.

Fowler, Edward. *Say'ya Blues: Laboring Life in Contempory Tokyo*. Ithaca, NY: Cornell University Press, 1996.

Gerlach, Michael L. *Alliance Capitalism: The Social Organization of Japanese Business*. Berkeley: University of California Press, 1992.

Gerth, Hans; and C. Wright Mills. *From Max Weber: Essays in Sociology*. New York: Oxford University Press, 1946.

Gibney, Frank. *The Pacific Century*. New York: Random House, 1992.

————. *Japan: The Fragile Super Power*. Revised ed. Tokyo: Tuttle, 1995.

Gluck, Carol. *Japan's Modern Myths: Ideology in the Late Meiji Period*. Princeton, NJ: Princeton University Press, 1985.

Goffman, Erving. *The Presentation of Self in Everyday Life*. Garden City, NY: Doubleday, 1959.

————. *Behavior in Public Places*. New York: Free Press, 1963.

————. *Interaction Ritual: Essays on Face-to-Face Behavior*. Garden City, NY: Doubleday, 1967.

Golzio, Karl Heinz. "Max Weber on Japan: The Role of the Government and the Buddhist Sects." In *Max Weber in Asian Studies*, ed. Andreas E. Buss, pp. 90–101. Leiden, Germany: E.J. Brill, 1985.

Gouldner, Alvin. *For Sociology: Renewal and Critique in Sociology Today*. New York: Basic Books, 1973.

Gouldner, Alvin; and Richard A. Peterson. *Notes on Technology and the Moral Order*. Indianapolis: Bobbs-Merrill, 1962.

Halliday, Jon. *A Political History of Japanese Capitalism*. New York: Monthly Review Press, 1975.

Hamabata, Matthews Masayuki. *Crested Kimono: Power and Love in the Japanese Business Family*. Ithaca, NY: Cornell University Press, 1990.

Hampden-Turner, Charles; and Alfons Trompenaars. *The Seven Cultures of Capitalism*. New York: Doubleday, 1993.

Hane, Mikiso. *Peasants, Rebels, and Outcastes: The Underside of Modern Japan*. New York: Pantheon, 1982.

————. *Reflections on the Way to the Gallows: Voices of Japanese Rebel Women*. New York: Pantheon, 1988.

Harada, Norio. "Nihon no Meimon Kurabu" (Prestigious clubs of Japan). In Jimbutsu Ōrai *Who's Who*, pp. 151–58. Tokyo: Shinjimbutsu Oraisha, 1988.

Hayakawa, Takashi. *Nihon no Jōryū Shakai to Keibatsu* (Japan's upper strata social groups and their family connections). Tokyo: Kodakawa Shoten, 1983.

Heise, David; Gerhard Lenski; and John Wardwell. "Further Notes on Technology and the Moral Order." *Social Forces* 55 (1976), pp. 316–37.

Hendry, Joy. *Understanding Japanese Society*. London: Croom Helm, 1987.

Herrnstein, Richard; and Charles Murray. *The Bell Curve: Intelligence and Class Structure in American Life*. New York: Free Press, 1994.

Hoffmeister, Gerhart; and Frederic C. Tubach. *Germany: 2000 Years: From the Nazi Era to German Unification*. Vol. III. New York: Continuum, 1992.

Hofstede, Geert. *Cultures and Organization: Software of the Mind*. New York: McGraw-Hill, 1991.

Ishida, Hiroshi. *Social Mobility in Contemporary Japan*. Palo Alto, CA: Stanford University Press, 1993.

Ishida, Hiroshi; John H. Goldthorpe; and Robert Erikson. "Intergenerational Class Mobility in Postwar Japan." *American Journal of Sociology* 96 (1991), pp. 954–93.

Jamieson, Neil L. *Understanding Vietnam*. Berkeley: University of California Press, 1995.

Jin, Ikko. *Keibatsu: Shin Tokuken Kaikyū no Keifu* (Genealogy of the new privileged class). Tokyo: Mainichi Shimbunsha, 1989.

Johnson, Chalmers. *MITI and the Japanese Miracle*. Stanford: Stanford University Press, 1982.

————. *Japan: Who Governs?* New York: Norton, 1995.

Kakuma, Takashi. *Nihon no Shihai Kaikyū, Jokan* (Japan's ruling class, part one). Tokyo: PHP Kenkujo, 1981.

Kallenberg, Arne L.; and James R. Lincoln. "The Structure of Earnings Inequality in the United States and Japan." *American Journal of Sociology* 94 (1988), pp. 5121–53.

Kamm, Henry. *Dragon Ascending: Vietnam and the Vietnamese.* New York: Arcade, 1996.

Kanter, Rosabeth Moss. *Commitment and Community.* Cambridge, MA: Harvard University Press, 1972.

Kaplan, David; and Alec Dubro. *Yakuza.* London: Futura, 1986.

Kaplan, David; and Andrew Marshall. *The Cult at the End of the World.* New York: Crown Books, 1996.

Keizai Koho. *Japan 1995: An International Comparison.* Tokyo: Keizai Koho Center (Japan Institute for Social and Economic Affairs), 1995.

Kerbo, Harold R. "A Sociology of Higher Education: Japanese University in the Context of Japanese Culture, Social Organization, and Social Stratification." *Sociological View Points* 10 (1994), pp. 66–78.

───────. *Social Stratification and Inequality: Class Conflict in Historical and Comparative Perspective.* 3rd ed. New York: McGraw-Hill, 1996.

Kerbo, Harold R.; and John McKinstry. *Who Rules Japan?: The Inner Circles of Economic and Political Power.* Westport, CT: Greenwood/Praeger, 1995.

Kerbo, Harold R.; and Keiko Nakao. "Corporate Structure and Modernization: A Comparative Analysis of Japan and the United States." *International Review of Sociology* 3 (1991), pp. 149–74.

Kerbo, Harold R.; and Robert Slagter. *Japanese and American Corporations in Thailand: Work Organization, Employee Relations, and Cultural Contrasts.* Unpublished manuscript, 1996.

Kerbo, Harold R.; and Elke Wittenhagen. "Asia and Western Theories of Social Stratification: Conceptual Universals or Western Bias?" Paper presented at the meetings of the International Sociological Association Research Committee on Social Stratification, Trento, Italy, May 1992.

Kerbo, Harold R.; Elke Wittenhagen; and Keiko Nakao. "Japanese Transplant Corporations, Foreign Employees, and the German Economy: A Comparative Analysis of Germany and the United States." *Duisburger Bettrage zur Soziologischen Forschung*, 1994.

Kishimoto, Kōichi. *Politics in Modern Japan: Development and Organization.* Tokyo: Japan Echo Inc., 1988.

Kitagawa, Takayoshi; and Kainuma Jun. *Nihon no Eriito* (Japan's elite). Tokyo: Otsuki Shoten, 1985.

Koh, B.C. *Japan's Administrative Elite.* Berkeley: University of California Press, 1989.

Lee, Changsoo; and George De Vos. *Koreans in Japan: Ethnic Conflict and Accommodation.* Berkeley: University of California Press, 1981.

Lenski, Gerhard. *Power and Privilege*. New York: McGraw-Hill, 1966.

_____ . "Marxist Experiments in Destratification: An Appraisal." *Social Forces* 57 (1978), pp. 364–83.

Lenski, Gerhard; Jean Lenski; and Partick D. Nolan. *Human Societies: An Introduction to Macrosociology*. 6th ed. New York: McGraw-Hill, 1991.

Lenski, Gerhard; and Patrick Nolan. "Trajectories of Development: A Further Test." *Social Forces* 64 (1986), pp. 794–95.

Lincoln, Edward J. *Japan: Facing Economic Maturity*. Washington, DC: The Brookings Institution, 1988.

Lincoln, James R.; Michael Gerlach; and Christina Ahmadjian. "Keiretsu Networks and Corporate Performance in Japan." *American Sociological Review* 61 (1996), pp. 67–88.

Lincoln, James R.; and Arne L. Kallenberg. "Work Organiztion and Work Force Commitment: A Study of Plants and Employees in the U.S. and Japan." *American Sociological Review* 50 (1985), pp. 738–50.

Lincoln, James R.; Arne L. Kallenberg; Michael Gerlach; and Peggy Takahashi. "Keiretsu Networks in the Japanese Economy: A Dyad Analysis of Intercorporate Ties." *American Sociological Review* 57 (1992), pp. 561–85.

_____ . *Culture, Control, and Commitment: A Study of Work Organization and Work Attitudes in the United States and Japan*. New York: Cambridge University Press, 1990.

Harold Kerbo; and Elke Wittenhagen. "Japanese Companies in Germany: A Case Study in Cross-Cultural Management." *Journal of Industrial Relations*, Spring 1995.

Long, Susan Orpett. "Nurturing and Femininity: The Ideal of Caregiving in Postwar Japan." In *Re-Imaging Japanese Women*, ed. Anne E. Imamura, pp. 156–76. Berkeley: University of California Press, 1996.

Massarella, Derek. *A World Elsewhere: Europe's Encounter with Japan in the Sixteenth and Seventeenth Centuries*. New Haven: Yale University Press, 1990.

McKinstry, John; and Asako McKinstry. *Jinsei Annai:"Life's Guide," Glimpses of Japan through a Popular Advice Column*. Armonk, NY: M.E. Sharpe, 1990.

Mills, C. Wright. *The Power Elite*. New York: Oxford University Press, 1956.

Minear, Richard H. "Orientalism and the Study of Japan." *Journal of Asian Studies* 30 (1980), pp. 507–17.

Mishel, Lawrence; and Jared Bernstein. *The State of Working America, 1992–1993*. Armonk, NY: M.E. Sharpe/Economic Policy Institute, 1993.

Miyake, Ichiro; Watakuki Jōji; Shima Sumi; and Urashima Ikuo. *Byōdō o Meguru Eriito to Taikō* (Equality, the elite, and the counterelite). Tokyo: Sobunsha, 1985.

Moore, Barrington. *Social Origins of Dictatorship and Democracy: Lord and Peasant in the Making of the Modern World*. Boston: Beacon, 1966.

Morgan, S. Philip; and Kiyosi Hirosima. "The Persistence of Extended Family Residence in Japan: Anachronism or Alternative Strategy." *American Sociological Review* 48 (1983), pp. 269–81.

Morikawa, Hidemasa. *Zaibatsu: The Rise and Fall of Family Enterprise Groups in Japan*. Tokyo: Tokyo University Press, 1992.

Morioka, Koji. "Japan." In *The Capitalist Class: An International* Study, ed. Tom Bottomore and Robert J. Brym, pp. 140–76. New York: New York University Press, 1989.

Mouer, Ross, and Yoshio Sugimoto. *Images of Japanese Society*. London: Kegan Paul International, 1986.

Muller, Edward. "Income Inequality, Regime Repressiveness, and Political Violence." *American Sociological Review* 50 (1985), pp. 47–61.

Nakane, Chie. *Japanese Society*. Berkeley: University of California Press, 1970.

Naoi, Atsushi; and Fumiaki Ojima. "Industrialization and Social Stratification: Reexamination of Treiman's Industrialization Thesis." Paper presented at the meetings of Research Stratification Committee of the International Sociological Association, Stanford, CA, August 1989.

Ohnuki-Tierney, Emiko. *Rice as Self: Japanese Identities through Time*. Princeton, NJ: Princeton University Press, 1993.

Okumura, Hiroshi. *Kigyō Shūdan no Keieisha* (Leaders in an era of industrial groups). Tokyo: Nikei Shinsha, 1978.

————— . *Shin-Nihon no Roku Dai Kigyō Shūdan* (Six great industrial groups of latter-day Japan). Tokyo: Daiyamondosha, 1983.

Ōsono, Tomokazu. *Kigyō Keiretsu to Gyōkai Chizu* (Map of industrial keiretsu and other big business circles). Tokyo: Nihon Jitsugyo Shuppansha, 1991.

Pempel, T. J. "Prerequisites for Democracy: Political and Social Institutions." In *Democracy in Japan*, ed. Takeshi Ishida and Ellis S. Krauss, pp. 17–38. Pittsburgh: Pittsburgh University Press, 1989.

Pharr, Susan J. *Losing Face: Status Politics in Japan*. Berkeley: University of California Press, 1990.

Price, John. *Japan Works: Power and Paradox in Postwar Industrial Relations*. Ithaca, NY: Cornell University Press, 1997.

Pye, Lucian W. *Asian Power and Politics: The Cultural Dimensions of Authority*. Cambridge, MA: Belknap/Harvard University Press, 1985.

Rauch, Jonathan. *The Outnation: A Search for the Soul of Japan*. Boston, MA: Harvard Business School Press, 1992.

Reischauer, Edwin O. *The Japanese*. Cambridge, MA: Harvard University Press, 1988.

Reischauer, Edwin O.; and Albert M. Craig. *Japan: Tradition and Transformation*. New York: Houghton Mifflin, 1978.

Reischauer, Edwin O.; and Marius B. Jansen. *The Japanese Today: Change and Continuity*. Cambridge, MA: Belknap/ Harvard University Press, 1995.

Roberts, John G. *Mitsui: Three Centuries of Japanese Business*. New York: Weatherhill, 1976.

Rohlen, Thomas P. *Japan's High Schools*. Berkeley: University of California Press, 1983.

Rosenbaum, James; and Takehiko Kariya. "From High School to Work: Market and Institutional Mechanisms in Japan." *American Journal of Sociology* 94 (1989), pp. 1334–65.

Rosenfeld, Eva. "Social Stratification in a 'Classless' Society." *American Sociological Review* 16 (1951), pp. 766–74.

Rosenstone, Robert A. *Mirror in the Shrine: American Encounters with Meiji Japan*. Cambridge, MA: Harvard University Press, 1988.

Sahara, Makoto. *Nihon no Rekishi I, Nihon no Tanjoo* (History of Japan, part I: Birth of the Japanese race). Tokyo: Dagakukan, 1987.

Sansom, G. B. *Japan: A Short Cultural History*. London: Barrie and Jenkins Ltd, 1958.

Sato, Ikuya. *Kamikaze Biker: Parody and Anonymity in Affluent Japan*. Chicago: University of Chicago Press, 1991.

Sato, Tomiyasu. *Monbatsu* (Family cliques). Tokyo: Rippu Shobu, 1987.

Schaede, Ulrike. "The 'Old Boy' Network and Government-Business Relationships in Japan." *Journal of Japanese Studies* 21 (1995), pp. 293–318.

Shapiro, Andrew L. *We're Number One: Where America Stands—and Falls—in the New World Order*. New York: Vintage Books, 1992.

Sherif, Muzafer. *In Common Predicament: Social Psychology of Intergroup Conflict and Cooperation*. Boston: Houghton Mifflin, 1996.

Shinnosuke, Inami. "Going After the Yakuza." *Japan Quarterly* 39 (1992), pp. 353–58.

Simmel, Georg. *Conflict and the Web of Group Affiliations*. Ed. Kurt Wolff and Reinhard Bendix. New York: Free Press, 1905/1955.

Skocpol, Theda. *States and Social Revolutions: A Comparative Analysis of France, Russia and China*. New York: Cambridge University Press, 1979.

Smith, Robert J. *Japanese Society: Tradition, Self, and the Social Order*. Cambridge: Cambridge University Press, 1983.

Spiro, Melford. *Kibbutz: Venture in Utopia*. New York: Schocken Books, 1970.

Stevenson, David Lee; and David P. Baker. "Shadow Education and Allocation in Formal Schooling: Transition to University in Japan." *American Journal of Sociology* 97 (1992), pp. 1639–57.

Thelen, Kathleen A. *Union of Parts: Labor Politics in Postwar Germany*. Ithaca, NY: Cornell University Press, 1991.

Thurow, Lester. *Head to Head: The Coming Economic Battle between the United States, Japan, and Europe*. New York: Morrow, 1991.

Tolbert, Charles; Patrick Horan; and E. M. Beck. "The Structure of Economic Segmentation: A Dual Economy Approach." *American Journal of Sociology* 85 (1980), pp. 1095–116.

Turner, Lowell. *Democracy at Work: Changing World Markets and the Future of Labor Unions*. Ithaca, NY: Cornell University Press, 1992.

Usui, Chikako; and Richard Colignon. "Amakudari: The Cement between the Japanese Polity and Economy." Paper presented at the annual meeting of the Midwest Sociological Society, St. Louis, MO, 1994.

van Wolferen, Karel. *The Enigma of Japanese Power*. New York: Knopf, 1989.

Varley, H. Paul. *Japanese Culture: A Short History*. New York: Holt, Rinehart and Winston, 1977.

Verba, Sidney, et al. *Elites and the Idea of Equality*. Cambridge, MA: Harvard University Press, 1987.

Vogel, Ezra. *Japan's New Middle Class*. Berkeley: University of California Press, 1971.

————— . *Japan as Number One: Lessons for America*. Cambridge, MA: Harvard University Press, 1979.

————— . *The Four Little Dragons: The Spread of Industrialization in East Asia*. Cambridge, MA: Harvard University Press, 1991.

Wallerstein, Immanual. *The Modern World System: Capitalist Agriculture and the Origins of the European World-Economy in the 16th Century*. New York: Academic Press, 1974.

————— . *The Modern World System II: Mercantilism and the Consolidation of the European World-Economy, 1600–1750*. New York: Academic Press, 1980.

————— . *The Modern World System III: The Second Era of Great Expansion of the Capitalist World-Economy, 1730–1840s*. New York: Academic Press, 1989.

Weber, Max. *From Max Weber: Essays in Sociology*. Ed. H. H. Gerth and C. Wright Mills. New York: Oxford University Press, 1946.

————— . *The City*. New York: Free Press, 1958.

White, Merry. *The Japanese Educational Challenge*. New York: Free Press, 1987.

Williams, Kirk. "Economic Sources of Homicide: Reestimating the Effects of Poverty and Inequality." *American Sociological Review* 49 (1984), pp. 283–89.

Wittfogel, Karl A. *Oriental Despotism: A Comparative Study of Total Power*. New Haven: Yale University Press, 1957.

Woodiwiss, Anthony. *Law, Labour and Society in Japan: From Repression to Reluctant Recognition*. London: Routledge, 1992.

Woronoff, Jon. *Politics the Japanese Way*. Tokyo: Lotus Press, 1986.

————— . *The Coming Social Crisis*. Tokyo: Lotus Press, 1980.

Yawata, Yasusada. "Religionssoziologisch Untersuchungen zur Geschichte Japans." In *Max Weber zum Gedachtnis*, ed. Rene Konig and Johannes Winckelmann. Koln/Opiaden: Westdeutscher Veriag (Kolner Zeitschrift fur Soziologie and Sozial-psychologie, Sonderheft 7), 1963.

amakudari   Literally, "descend from heaven," referring to either of two phenomena: (1) A high-ranking officer at a public agency or large corporation who retired from his main career to become the figurehead president of a smaller enterprise. (2) A person in mid-career at one of the national ministries who quits to join a corporation that is regulated by the ministry at which he or she formerly served.

Aum Shinrikyō   Something like "True Knowledge Church of Oum," this religious cult was started by a legally blind but highly charismatic man named Matsushita Shizuo, or as Americans would put it, Shizuo Matsushita. As the cult began to grow in size in the 1980s, Matsushita changed his name to the more elegant sounding Asahara Shoko. It has always been a highly secretive organization, eventually developing bizarre ideas of taking over control of the nation, and even the world. Some of the people who joined the cult were highly educated and had sophisticated technical skills, allowing the cult to experiment with all kinds of lethal concoctions. After releasing poison gas in two subway cars near the center of Tokyo, the cult was eventually disbanded by Japanese authorities and the leaders put on trial. As this is written the trials have not concluded.

bōsōzoku   "Violent drivers," originally referring to young men who drive motorcycles and cars with great noise and abandon late at night. The term is used more loosely now to refer to other kinds of youth gangs.

Burakumin   Japan's population of from two to three million outcastes. As the text suggests, their origin is clouded; some of the popular explanations of how they came to be an outcaste group have proven to be untrue. Historically Burakumin have suffered from severe discrimination, though no intrinsic characteristic distinguishes them from other Japanese.

chikan   Men who molest women with probing hands in Japan's crowded public transportation environment.

daimyo   The head of feudal han or fiefs in the Japanese system of feudal estates from around AD 1000 until the han system was abolished early in the Meiji period after 1868. In earlier times, daimyo were like kings of small kingdoms, but under the Tokugawa shogunate much of their power was regulated by the central government.

danchi   This refers both to resident-owned apartments, relatively small, usually constructed of steel and concrete, and to the apartment complexes made up of the individual units. Some danchi contain as few as 20 units, but some close to large metropolitan areas are immense with literally thousands of units consisting of dozens of separate buildings with its own shopping center and central park area.

Diet   A word of Latin derivation used in Western languages to refer to the two houses of the Japanese national legislative body. It is used in Japan only when people speak or write in foreign languages. The Japanese name for the national legislature is *koku gikai*.

Edo   Originally a village near the mouth of a river of the same name at the head of a natural bay along the eastern coast. Edo was suddenly elevated in importance when the great warlord Ieyasu Tokugawa chose to rule Japan as shogun from a palace complex he began to construct just a few kilometers from the village shortly after he took power in 1600. Due to the hostage system, the *sankin kōtai*, warlords from all over Japan were forced to live near the palace, and within 50 years Edo had spread around the palace and become a good-size city. By 1750 it had grown into one of the largest cities in the world. When the Tokugawa regime was finally overthrown in 1868, the new rulers of Japan decided to move the Emperor from his residence in Kyoto to Edo and make the latter the legal as well as de facto capital, which it had been for more than 250 years. It was then that the name Edo was changed to its present name, Tokyo, "eastern capital."

gakureki   The system of determining the worth of people according to the rank of the university they attended. In contemporary Japan the term is usually used in a negative context as part of criticism of what many both in and out of Japan consider to be an excessive amount of pressure put on young people to pass entrance examinations to enter prestigious universities.

genkan   The area of a private residence immediately inside the main door to the outside. It is at ground level and in a way considered part of the outside. Anyone can enter the genkan—salespersons, police, delivery service people—but beyond the genkan is the oku, the very private area of the house where only intimate friends and relatives normally go.

han   A Japanese feudal estate, similar in meaning to the way *fief* is used in describing European feudalism. During Japan's feudal period, roughly mid-1400s to the middle of the nineteenth century, han varied in number from a little more than 100 to over 250 and varied in size from only a few thousand acres to several hundred square miles.

honne   How things "really are," as opposed to a social fiction, referred to as *tatemae*. For example, in determining whether the person listed as the chief executive officer of a private company is really the person with the greatest power in the company would depend on whether the title is honne, an actual description of the person's power, or tatemae, a title conferring status but no real power.

ie   The Japanese version of the agrarian extended family. Like extended families in other traditional societies, ie was patrilineal and patrilocal for the main family heir.

juku   An old term originally referring to the training institutes where young samurai were given lessons in Confucionist doctrine and other academic subjects. Since the 1950s it has come to refer to supplemental schooling as an aid in preparing young people for high school and university entrance examinations, and to the places where the schooling takes place. Juku vary in size and formality from merely a room in a teacher's house to very large building complexes larger than some high schools. Juku classes begin in late afternoon after regular school ends and continue for many students on Saturday and even Sunday.

kami   In Japanese animism this term referred to the various spirits and local gods that made up original Shinto. It is still used in this way, but in recent centuries kami has come to be associated with a more general sense of divine or supernatural force.

Kansai   The land area in southwestern Honshu (the largest main island of Japan) around the northern part of Osaka Bay, which includes the urban regions of Osaka, Kobe, and the area inland as far as Kyoto. Kansai has its own accent and for many a special identity.

Kanto   The large area roughly 50 miles from north to south and 75 miles from east to west surrounding Tokyo and extending to the mountains north and west of the capital. Kanto includes of course the special capital district as well as parts of five prefectures, with a total population of nearly 20 million.

karōshi   The three Chinese characters used to write this term spell out "excessive work death," implying death from overwork. Various symptoms leading to the death of male white-collar workers have been attributed to stress produced by work in recent years, with estimates as high as 10,000 victims per year.

kazoku   The word that most closely translates to the English word *family*. It is actually a relatively recent development in Japan and stands in contrast to the more traditional ie.

keibatsu   Networks formed through marriage. The term is used almost exclusively to refer to the extended family ties through marriage among people of power and prestige, forming a basis of elite community that protects and furthers mutual interests.

Keidanren   A private organization of about 1,000 industrial leaders that could best be described as a congress of industrial leaders. It has no official governmental function, but its ties with political leaders are so close, and the overall financial power it represents is so overwhelming, that it has come to have enormous influence in economic planning for the nation.

keiretsu   Groups of private companies with informal ties and agreements of cooperation at the top of the Japanese business world. Keiretsu represent a partial revival of the old zaibatsu system of prewar Japan, but without the role played by the founding family and with more freedom to do business outside the group.

Meiji   The historical period in Japan from 1868–1912. It is the reign name of Emperor Mutsuhito, the first emperor ever to reside in Tokyo. The term *Meiji* is associated with Japan's period of rapid modernization following the forced isolation of the long Edo period.

omiai   An arranged meeting for purposes of determining if two people will find themselves mutually compatible for marriage. Omiai are highly formalized and usually take place in private rooms of restaurants. Parents are usually in attendance and the whole affair lasts an hour or so. If both parties agree, courtship normally begins after the omiai, but either party can end the relationship after the first meeting with no feelings of embarrassment.

rōnin   Originally this term referred to unattached samurai who for some reason had lost the sponsorship of their feudal master, sometimes because their han was destroyed in warfare. Today the term is used for young people who have failed in their attempt to pass the entrance examination to the university of their dreams, and who sort of drop out of life, doing practically nothing but studying for the entire year until the next exam.

sakoku rei   The law promulgated by the Tokugawa regime in 1615 making it punishable by death for anyone to enter Japan and for any Japanese to attempt to leave. Japanese living overseas were given a grace period of a few years to return, and after that, Japan was quite literally sealed off from the outside world until the middle of the nineteenth century.

samurai   This term simply meant warrior or professional soldier in Japan until during the Edo period, when it actually became an official rank in a frozen Japanese caste system. From then until the end of the Tokugawa regime, samurai were born into their social position, and all males of the category were schooled in military arts and lived as a kind of parasite warrior caste.

sankin kōtai   The system devised by the Tokugawa regime to guarantee against military uprisings that had made continuity of military regimes impossible in the 200 years before the Tokugawa clan took control of the country in 1600. It was essentially a hostage system in which all warlords, or daimyo, were forced to live half of each year in the capital at Edo, and during the remaining half year, wives, parents, and other close relatives had to take their place. It was an ingenious system that not only stopped the civil wars, but proved to be a great urban development program for the area around the palace.

Shinto   The name given to the native nature worship system of Japanese religion. During the Edo period, there was an attempt to organize Shinto into a somewhat standardized theology to compete with Buddhism in prestige, and during the Meiji period, it was elevated to the position of a state religion. Today Shinto retains elements of its ancient past together with modernized forms to coexist with Buddhism as the main religious orientations of almost all Japanese.

shogun   Originally, *Tai I Dai Shogun*, something like "Barbarian subduing great generalissimo," it was a title invented in the seventh century for the head of the military forces deployed against the aboriginal population of the area north and east of Kyoto. It was revived in 1285 when a warlord by the name of Yoritomo Minamoto temporally gained control of most of the nation and ruled as shogun. Following that, the position of shogun became a hereditary title of the military man who in theory ruled Japan in the name of the emperor, but by the fourteenth century it had become more or less symbolic, without any real power. When Ieyasu Tokugawa took the title of shogun in 1600, it again came to signify the actual ruler of Japan, and his descendants ruled in turn as shogun until the office was abolished in 1868.

tatemae   This refers to formal fictions Japanese use in such things as bestowing rank to people in an honorary sense, without actually granting corresponding power and authority. One of the writers of this book was for a time the tatemae president of a small college in Tokyo, but in reality the title conferred no authority to make important decisions as to how the college was run.

Todai The abbreviation most Japanese use when referring to *Tokyo Daigaku*, or the University of Tokyo, the pinnacle of the Japanese world of higher education.

Tokugawa The surname of the family that ruled from Edo as shogun from 1600 until the end of the regime in 1868. There were 15 Tokugawa shogun in all, the first 3, Ieyasu, Hidetada, and Iemitsu, were actual rulers with great personal power, but as usually the case in Japan, the office of shogun soon reverted to a figurehead position, and under the remaining Tokugawa shogun, actual power was in the hands of ruling committees.

yakuza The Japanese version of organized crime gangs. In many ways yakuza are like the Mafia of the West. One difference is that yakuza operate much more in the open, with organizations listed in the telephone book and identifying signs over their headquarters. The main sources of income for yakuza are extortion and businesses such as prostitution and illegal gambling.

yoshi A man who takes the family name of his wife and becomes the legal heir of her father's estate.

zaibatsu Literally, "economic groups," the cartels that stood at the center of the Japanese economy from the late nineteenth century until the U.S. occupation authorities disbanded them at the end of World War II. There were four main zaibatsu—Mitsui, Mitsubishi, Yasuda, and Sumitomo—and several minor zaibatsu; each was headed by a main family that provided the nominal leadership; they grew to be some of the wealthiest families in the world. Major zaibatsu all had their own banks, trading companies, and manufacturing enterprises, and each controlled separate political parties. They were fierce competitors, enforcing exclusivity within the group, but occasionally could be induced to cooperate, as in the development of colonial areas such as Manchuria and Taiwan.

GLOSSARY OF
SOCIOLOGICAL TERMS

altruistic suicide   One of the four types in Émile Durkheim's typology of suicide. Altruistic suicide is associated with very strong group orientation and usually occurs either from a feeling of letting a group down by failing in some responsibility, or through sacrifice for a group. The other types of suicide are *egoistic*, caused mainly by social isolation; *anomic*, caused by dramatic change leaving people with a feeling that norms are meaningless; and *fatalistic*, the escape from physical or psychological pain.

bureaucracy   According to Max Weber, a form of rational social organization based on fixed, written rules and a hierarchy of positions; it has come to dominate in industrial societies.

capitalist development state   A capitalist industrialist economy wherein the state has extensive control in managing the economy with major policies oriented toward economic development.

caste system   A system of social stratification based on status rankings and strict ascription. It was found in its most complete sense in precolonized India, but many elements of a caste system were instituted in Japan during the Tokugawa period.

church   A religious organization widely accepted as legitimate and with values and practices that are seen as the normal way to practice religion in a given society.

class   In one of the most general definitions it is a grouping of individuals with similar positions and similar political and economic interests within the stratification system. According to Max Weber, it is a dimension of social stratification based on property ownership or the lack of ownership (as in Marxian theory) but also occupational skill level.

collectivist value system   A value system stressing that the group is more important than the individual and individual desires, requiring greater sacrifice for the group's interests.

cult   A religious organization, usually relatively small, with values and practices outside the norms of the society that it is in; it is not accepted as legitimate by average people.

culture   Culture can be most broadly defined as the learned part of human behavior. Culture is the blueprint for living, including rules for behavior called *norms*, as well as broader belief systems called *values*.

divination   The use of nonreligious supernatural forces to know things not knowable through ordinary sources. It is often used to gain some end or to protect from some danger.

dramaturgical theory The idea put forth by Irving Goffman and other sociologists that the theater can be a useful analogy for studying human behavior. Although Goffman did not apply this technique to understanding the Japanese, it may be especially useful in examining behavior in that society, where social roles are played at a somewhat more conscious level than is often the case elsewhere.

dual economy An economic structure in which a few huge corporations form a core of industries, such as the auto industry, petroleum industry, and so forth, while the rest of the economy—such as general merchandising, service stations, and restaurants—is on the economic periphery. Stability and working conditions are much more favorable in the core industries. Both Japan and the United States have been characterized this way, with Japan perhaps a more pure example.

ethnic group A group of people relatively distinct in cultural background compared to the dominant group in the society.

extended family A family grouping that consists of more than one generation with authority vested in the oldest members.

feudalism/estate system An agrarian system of social stratification based on land ownership with a high level of ascription.

forced industrialization A method of industrialization in which the state forces heavy investment in basic industries, with low wages to workers (usually peasants, as in Japan) so that all surplus profits can be reinvested for more rapid economic development.

gender Socially acquired and socially defined sex-linked behavior expectations in a particular society.

individualistic value system A value system stressing the greater importance of the individual and individual freedoms over group needs and restraints.

middle class Individuals and families with relatively little property, but high-to-middle positions in occupation (nonmanual labor) and authority. Further distinction is made with respect to the upper-middle class (lesser corporate managers, doctors, lawyers, and so forth) and lower-middle class (office workers, clerks, salespeople).

multidimensional view of social stratification The perspective originated by Max Weber that argues that Marx's view of ownership versus nonownership of the means of production as the most important dimension of social stratification is too simple. Rather, Weber stressed that class, status, and power (or party) can be important dimensions behind stratification systems.

patrilineal A system of tracing descent through the male line and of inheriting property and family identity exclusively through one's father.

power In the social stratification theories of Max Weber, power is defined as the ability to achieve goals in the face of opposition from others.

primary groups Small groups with relatively high levels of intimacy and informality. Most sociologists include family groups in the category, as well as groups of friends and other intimate associates. In the simplest hunter/gatherer and horticultural societies, the entire society is a primary group. In more complex societies, primary groups are formed within larger secondary groups.

racial group   A socially defined grouping of people assumed to have common biological characteristics that separate them from other people.

secondary groups   A larger group with a specialized purpose within which people interact on a more impersonal, role-related basis. Most secondary groups, like a sociology class, are limited in time; however, a few, like the Catholic Church, have survived for more than 1,000 years.

sect   A relatively small religious organization that either deviates from or actually opposes the teachings of mainstream religion, but which, unlike cults, is not normally secretive or seen as completely illegitimate by average people.

social institutions   An abstract way of defining the problem-solving groupings in society. Family, the economy, religion, polity (the way formal power is organized), criminal justice, and so forth are all abstractions, referring to the way energy is organized to deal with specific tasks faced by any society.

social mobility   Movement to a significant degree up or down within a system of social stratification. Social mobility is often divided into two types: *intergenerational* social mobility, movement up or down compared to one's parents, and *intragenerational* social mobility, movement up or down in one's own lifetime.

social problems   Situations and conditions defined as negative or harmful in the society. What comes to be defined as such is strongly influenced by those who have more power or influence within the society.

social stratification   The condition in which layered hierarchy and inequality have been hardened or *institutionalized,* and there is a *system of social relationships* that determines who gets what and why.

social structure   A system of social relations among individuals within groups and among groups or categories of people in the society. This is the network of social relations that are the building blocks of societies.

status   Basically this refers to the response given by others to the ranking, high or low, of any individual in a social hierarchy. Social status determines the level of respect and honor individuals commonly are accorded by others.

traditional authority   According to Weber, authority that rests on an established belief in the sanctity of immemorial traditions and the legitimacy of the status of those exercising authority under them.

upper class   Old, established families with significant ownership of major corporations and therefore extensive authority and economic power. Upper-class status in Japan was certainly held by the old zaibatsu of prewar Japan and those families given titles of the nobility after the Meiji Restoration.

INTERNET RESOURCES

Chapter 1: The Place, the People, and the Past

http://www.japan-guide.com/list/e1000.html   Guide to Japan. Information on regions, prefectures, area and locations, population, volcanos, earthquakes, climate, environment, statistics, census, factbook, and maps.

http://users.ccnet.com/~suntzu75/japemps.htm   A list of Japan's ruling emperors and eight ruling empresses from Jimmu 660 BC to Akihito AD 1996.

Chapter 2: Japanese Culture and Social Structure

http://www.try-net.or.jp/~kzuk/   Zuk Family Home Page. Various links to culture, politics, music, newspapers, magazines, food, geography, regional information, sports, and tourism.

Chapter 3: The Japanese Political System

http://www.daiwa-foundation.org.uk/politics.html   Japanese politics. Links to Japanese Communist Party, Liberal Democratic Party, New Party SAKIGAKE, Social Democratic Party, and various articles.

http://www.bekkoame.or.jp/~jneuffer/   "Behind the Screen: Roundup of Japanese Politics." Information and links to political parties, ministries and agencies, back issues of "Behind the Screen."

Chapter 4: The Japanese Economy

http://164.11.100.12/siv/htm/docs/japanl.htm   Various links to economic and business planning, banking, finance, forecasts, surveys, theory and research, and policy.

http://hoshi.cic.sfu.ca/forum/wright.html   "Networking in Japan: The Case of Keiretsu," by Dr. Richard W. Wright, McGill University and Willamette University. Topics include brief overviews of the background and characteristics of keiretsu; the integrating mechanisms of the keiretsu; the coordinating role of banks; Japan and North America: contrasts in meaning of financial terms, consequences for investors, business partners, and competitors; changes in the structure of Japanese companies today.

http://www.jetro.go.jp/Jetroinfo/Focusjapan/96-11.html   Keiretsu Supplier System Changing.

http://www. daiwa-foundation.org.uk/economy.html   Various links related to the economy and industry, Japanese business, economic trends, and Keidanren.

http://www.keidanren.or.jp/   Keidanren: Japanese Federation of Economic Organizations.

http://entrance.epa.go.jp/l/e-e/chart   Charts of Japanese economy.

http://www.japantimes.co.jp/features/feat4-96/holdb.html   Conglomerates—then and now. A brief timeline on conglomerates in Japan; source, *Japan Times*.

http://www.keidanren.or.jp/A2J/   Access to Japan. List of contact points for procurement. A large list of links to companies and industries.

Chapter 5: Social Stratification in Japan

http://risya3.hus.osaka-u.ac.jp/shigeto/ssm/ssmE.html   Survey on Social Stratification and Social Mobility (SSM).

Chapter 6: The Japanese Power Elite

http://www.mofa.go.jp/   The Ministry of Foreign Affairs of Japan.

http://www.sbpark.com/inn31.html   Global Cyber Business Park. Home pages of the Japanese Diet members, open forum on issues and policies. Lists education and political careers.

Chapter 7: The Family

http://kgu-web.kansai-gaidai-u.ac.jp/bekka/student/gaic9.html   Living with a Japanese family. Guidelines on Japanese etiquette on the home, toilet, daily schedule, meals, heating, bath, laundry, privacy, helping around the house, and polite forms.

Chapter 8: Religion

http://www.io.com/~nishio/japan/religion.html   Short descriptions of several major religions in Japan, e.g., Shintoism, Buddhism; Jodo, Buddhism; Esoterics, Buddhism; Zen, Taoism, Onmyo-Do, Christianity.

http://www.ualberta.ca/~slis/guides/religion/buddhism.htm   Links to Buddhist literature, e.g., Tibetan, Vajrayana, Vietnamese, and Zen.

http://coombs.anu.edu.au/WWWVL-Buddhism.html   Buddhist Studies WWW Virtual Library. An Internet guide to Buddhism and Buddhist studies.

http://www.sokagakkai.or.jp/html3/index3.html   Soka Gakkai: A Buddhist association. News, viewpoints, culture, and education.

Chapter 9: Education

http://www.accessasia.com/xroad/xrjpedu.html Links to various universities, colleges, institutes of technology, high schools, junior high schools, and elementary schools.

Chapter 10: Cities

http://mai.hyg.med.kyoto-u.ac.jp/KansaiWWW/2.htmlKansai-WWW. Information for foreigners in Kansai.

Chapter 11: Social Problems in Modern Japan

http://welfare.or.kr/search/yahoodir.htm Yahoo directory. Links to topics on welfare in Japan.

http://www.ifnet.or.jp/~inoken/index_e.html Homelessness in Japan.

http://www.io.com/%7Enishio/japan/yakuza.html Yakuza: past and present (criminal gangs). Feudal Japan, modernization of the yakuza, occupation years, modern yakuza, and the yakuza in today's Japan.

http://133.91.192.47/fps93p/p9304003/www_docs/project2.htm Bullying in Japanese schools.

http://www.ces.kyutech.ac.jp/student/JapanEdge/e-index.html The Internet Edge Culture Archive of Japan ("Japan Edge"). Introduces Japanese street/underground culture information.

Chapter 12: Social Change and Japan in the Twenty-First Century

http://icg.stwing.upenn.edu/~konrad/jp.html Japan Information Resource Center. Information on business, culture, language, history, government, living in Japan, and more.

Miscellaneous

http://www.uiowa.edu/~caps/virtual_japan.html Web resources in Japan. Universities in Japan, government and ministry pages, and newspapers.

http://www.japan guide.com/ Guide to Japan. An excellent resource on the economy, history, living in Japan, politics, religion, society, and so forth (still under construction). Includes other links such as Japanese recipes and photography of interesting cities and scenes.

http://www.ntt.co.jp/SQUARE/www-in-JP.html Links to universities and businesses.

http://133.91.192.47/fps93p/p9304003/www_docs/project2.htm   Ask Asia.

Newspapers

http://www.japantimes.co.jp/home.html   *Japan Times.*
http://www.yomiuri.co.jp/   *Yomiuri Shimbun.*
http://www.yomiuri.co.jp/index-e.htm   *Yomiuri Shimbun.*
http://www.asahi.com/english/english.html   *Asahi Shimbun.*
http://www.mainichi.co.jp/index-e.html   *Mainichi Shimbun.*
http://oroppas.sec.or.jp/HomePage2.html   *Hokkaido Shimbun.*
http://www.kmt-iri.go.jp/index.html   *Kumamoto Shimbun.*
http://www.kyoto-np.co.jp/kp/index_e.html   *Kyoto Shimbun.*

Magazines

http://jmacsun.j-mac.co.jp/SJ/   *Saporro Journal.*
http://www.kyushu.com/gleaner.html   *Gaijin Gleaner.*

NAME INDEX

SUBJECT INDEX

Aging population, 162–164
Ainu, 4
Amakudari, 78–79
Article 9, Japanese
    Constitution, 43
Asahara, Shoko, 108–109
    and Aum Shinrikyō,
        108–109
    significance of, 109
Asian concept of power, 35
Asian value systems, 21–22
    origins, 22–23
Aum Shinrikyō cult, 166

Birth rates, 162–163
Bōsōzoku, 147–24
Buddhism, 100–103
    history in Japan, 102
    relationship to Shinto,
        100, 103
    role in funerals, 103–104
Burakumin, 69–71, 151–152
Business clubs, 80

Capitalist development
    state, 48
Caste system, 62
Chikan, 155
China, dynasties, 8
Christianity, in Japan, 12
    role of in Japan, 106
Citizen participation in
    government, 39–40
Class, 61
Collectivist value system,
    definition, 21
Conformity, 27
Confucianism, 87
Corporate stock
    ownership, 76
Crime, 144–146
    international
        comparisons, 145
Cultural traditions, 19
Culture, definition, 20

Daimyō, 11–12
Democratic Party, of
    Japan, 38

Diet, 34, 66, 77–78
    make-up, 37–38
    and money politics,
        40–41
Divination in Japan, 109
Dramaturgical theory,
    26–27
Drug abuse, 166
Dual economy, 52, 53
Durkheim, Emile, 22, 156

Edo, history of, 11
Edo period
    as center of Tokugawa
        regime, 12
    social system
        described, 12
    support in the legal
        system, 89
Elections, compared to
    U.S., 34
Elite unity, 78–81
    and *Amakudari*, 78–79
    and intermarriage, 81
    and "old school ties,"
        79–80
    and social clubs, 80
Ethnic inequalities, 67–68,
    150–153
Extended family,
    defined, 85

Family
    in history, 84
    influence of *ie* on
        courtship, 90
    patrilineal, 85
Feudalism, 35
Forced industrialization, 48
Freud, Sigmund, 22

Gender inequalities, 67–68
Genkan, 31
German works councils, 65
Giri, 29–30
Group conflicts, 25, 27–28

Hokkaido, compared to
    New England, 2

Honne, 26
Horizontal keiretsu, 51

Ie, characteristics of, 86
    defined, 85
    influence on
        courtship, 90
Income inequality,
    comparative, 62–64,
        169n
Income ratios, comparative,
    60, 169n
Individualism, radical, 168
Individualism index, 21
Individualistic value
    system, definition, 21
Industrial Revolution, 5, 14
In-group/ out-group, 28
Inside/outside, concept of,
    31–32
Interaction rituals, 26–27

Japanese
    attitude toward city
        life, 128
    borrowing from China,
        6–7
    bullying, 148–149
    castle towns, 129
    city life, positive aspects
        of, 132
    climate, 2
    corporate elite, 76–77
    corporations, 50–53,
        76–77
    company unions, 56
    crime, 144–146
    criminal justice system,
        146–147
    crowding, 2
    danchi, 131
    as a developed
        society, 4–5
    economic development,
        47–49
    economy and change, 53
    elections, 34, 38
    emperor, role of, 8–9

193

952.04   Kerbo, Harold R.
Ker

            Modern Japan.

DATE			
NOV 1 7 2000			
JUN 1 9 2001			
SEP 2 8 2001			
7/2/R			
11/12/03			
11/26/03			
3/18/04			